# THE ART OF INQUIRY

Sharon Smith

# The Art of Inquiry

## Questioning Strategies for K–6 Classrooms

Nancy Lee Cecil

PEGUIS
PUBLISHERS

Winnipeg   Manitoba   Canada

Printed and bound in Canada by Hignell Printing Limited


95   96   97   98   99   5   4   3   2   1


**Canadian Cataloguing in Publication Data**

Cecil, Nancy Lee

    The art of inquiry

    Includes bibliographical references.
    ISBN 1-895411-74-2

1. Questioning. 2. Teaching. 3. Learning. I. Title

LB1027.44.C43   1995      371.3'7   C95-920015-0


Book and Cover Design: Laura Ayers

Peguis Publishers
100–318 McDermot Avenue
Winnipeg, MB
Canada R3A 0A2
toll free 1-800-667-6793

To Dr. George Brandon,
for his interest in who I am and what I do.

# CONTENTS

# ACKNOWLEDGMENTS

This book maintains that the art of questioning is a very exciting form of social interaction; in many ways, so too is writing a book about questioning. I must acknowledge the valuable interaction of the many colleagues and students who have shared their ideas and experiences with me during my years at California State University. These people are too numerous to mention by name, but their voices, spirit, and even work samples are reflected throughout this book.

I would also like to thank my editor, Leigh Hambly, for her considerable skill in bringing this book to print, for handling all the nasty details, and for actually caring about the book as much as I do. Thanks also go to the wonderful folks at Peguis for their unfailing support in every phase of production of this book.

Finally, I must express my gratitude to my husband, Gary, and my beautiful daughter, Chrissy, for their infinite patience and support, even when all of life revolved around my writing.

. . . .

EDITOR'S NOTE

One of the dilemmas facing today's editor is that of retaining writing clarity while ensuring gender balance. This relates specifically to the use of the personal pronouns he/she, him/her, himself/herself, and so on. Using both forms in all cases makes for particularly awkward reading. In this book, we have chosen to use masculine pronouns in reference to students and feminine pronouns in reference to teachers. We assure the reader that no affront is intended in any way.

. . . .

# INTRODUCTION

Why do people choose to become teachers? Having read, through the years, the professional goal statements of hundreds of eager students entering the field of education, I am amazed at how many mention "the excitement of seeing a light bulb go on in a little head when that child suddenly understands a concept or an idea." Most present and future teachers, it seems, are attracted to the profession not by the modest salary, but by the promise of those blissful moments when a child under their tutelage appears to have *learned*. Often, it's children's answers to questions about what they are reading or studying that are taken as the evidence that this learning has, indeed, taken place.

And that is the premise of this book: asking just the right questions of elementary-age children is directly related to these heady instances of sudden understanding. Throughout, the preservice and practicing teacher will discover numerous ideas about how to model provocative, open-ended questions and how to help children learn to ask their own critical questions about content.

## HOW TO USE THIS BOOK

This book is divided into two sections. In Part I, I describe the taxonomy of questions, their uses, and the environmental factors necessary for the free flow of questions and answers in the classroom. I explore the types of questions that teachers can ask; a definition, description, and an example of each are presented. A self-check is also included so that teachers can determine their ability to identify the various levels of questions and, perhaps, begin asking more questions of a critical or open-ended nature.

Then I focus on the ideal environment for questioning: how to create a classroom climate in which children feel free to ask and answer questions, where they feel competent to ask about topics that interest them, and where they can work with one another to investigate issues. There are also caveats about common practices that tend to squelch creative and critical thinking thereby thwarting question asking and answering.

In Part II, I address specific questioning strategies that teachers can use to ask more thought-provoking questions, thus enhancing their students' construction of meaning from text and critical thinking. Next, I give suggestions and provide strategies that show teachers how to enable their students to generate their *own* questions. Then, I show how questioning strategies can be integrated across the entire curriculum, and examine strategies particularly appropriate for math, science, social studies, and art appreciation.

Finally, for those teachers who are interested in reading more about questioning techniques and critical thinking I have included an extensive bibliography of books, articles, and papers on those topics.

## WHO THIS BOOK IS FOR

This book is for teachers of grades K–6 who are already convinced magic can occur when one has asked just the right kinds of questions. Such teachers want to develop their questioning skills to a level where their students are noticeably more involved in the learning process.

This book is also for all the preservice teachers who still fantasize about the joy they will experience when they see *the light bulb go on.* When teachers ask the right questions of their students, they stimulate in-depth thinking and invite sudden connections and insights. It is in the classes of such teachers that light bulbs can be observed going on in young heads—all day long.

# PART I

# THE IMPORTANCE
# OF GOOD QUESTIONS

J ust how important are questions in the academic life of a child? According to Sigel and Saunders (1979), questioning is critical because it requires children to distance themselves in time and space from the present. Sigel (1982: 50) defines distancing as the "psychological separation of [the student] from the immediate, on-going present." When responding to questions about past or future events, the child shifts from the present to another, distant mode of thought, rather than simply basing a response on currently observable events. Thinking about past or future events requires an abstract mental representation of what has happened or of what may soon happen to the child. This ability to abstract calls for a higher plane of thinking that results, ultimately, in increased learning.

Asking questions also appears to be an effective way to direct and develop reading comprehension in children, especially when the teacher models good questions and shows children how to ask their *own* questions. Asking one's own questions is a form of making predictions and is essential to comprehension—it forces one to *construct* meaning rather than passively accept text as it is encountered. Children who are good predictors—and therefore good self-questioners—are also good comprehenders of text (Kestler 1992).

Finally, imagination can be enhanced only when children are given the opportunity to play with ideas, to discover relationships, and, most important, to ask questions. If, as educators, we demonstrate to children that their ideas have value and that their questions will be carefully considered, we are adding a rich source of fuel to children's motivation for learning. Children who are encouraged to ask and answer carefully crafted questions are being given an opportunity to explore with their minds, to gain meaning for themselves, and to relate new data to old ideas. And when children seek to ask or answer questions about things or events for which there is no one right answer (or are many potentially correct answers), they begin to develop an attitude of appreciation for the immensity and complexity of the natural world. *This* is when true learning begins to take place within and beyond the classroom doors!

## WHAT ARE THE *RIGHT* QUESTIONS?

Most teachers believe that asking children questions facilitates learning and cognitive development of learners. It is not surprising, therefore, that over 50 percent of adult verbal interactions with young children are composed of adult questions (Blank & Allen 1976). Studies involving elementary-school teachers reveal that they ask about 3.5 questions per minute, with teachers asking approximately twenty-seven questions for every pupil question (Floyd 1960). To improve the *quality* of the questions teachers ask, it helps to examine the *types* of questions asked, their impact on children's learning, and the teacher's role in facilitating that learning. From this information, helpful strategies and techniques for asking questions can be developed.

Current research on questioning suggests that teachers are *not* asking enough of the kinds of open-ended questions that enhance a child's imagination and facilitate critical thinking. Bromley (1992: 139) draws the following conclusions:

+ Seventy-five percent of the questions teachers ask are of a factual or literal nature.
+ Over 50 percent of the questions contained in the basal readers, still pervasively used in elementary schools, are of a factual or literal nature.
+ Teachers ask an average of seventy literal or factual questions in an average thirty-minute lesson.

D. Thomas (1988: 555) reminds us that children have a universal, inquisitive nature, and that they are continually asking questions to learn or to challenge ideas. However, she argues, without the open-ended *why* questions, the *what*s and the *how*s that generally precede factual questions will not really matter very much to children. Neither the question nor the answer will draw the child in, or engage his mind in a meaningful way. The *why* questions, she avows, are critical because they jump to "the very heart of learning: the spirit of curiosity, the purpose for which we get up a school system at all, the reasons we teach."

## THE LIMITATIONS OF FACTUAL QUESTIONS

Why do most teachers ask so many factual questions? Teachers may believe that factual questions are easier to answer because only small amounts of specific information are needed to answer them. But this is not so. A child with good critical-thinking skills may know all about Columbus's difficulties securing support for his explorations from Italian, Spanish, and Portuguese royalty, but be unable to remember the exact year Columbus "discovered" America. Teachers may also believe there are fewer possible answers to dispute with factual questions than there are with interpretive or evaluative questions (which often involve background knowledge or personal opinion). But by responding only to factual questions, students miss out on the critical and creative thinking benefits that derive from rigorous discussion. Finally, some teachers may emphasize factual questions because such questions require concise answers. Teachers may think that classroom behavior may be more easily controlled when many children are involved in fast-paced question and answering. If this is the case, the teacher is inviting children to become superficially involved in an *inquisition*, but never actively engaged in *inquiry*.

What subtle message does the teacher who asks mainly factual questions give her students? Children may get the impression facts and details are more important than personal interpretations or evaluations of events and ideas. They may feel they are not intelligent if they happen to have short-term memories and ignore names and dates, for example, in favor of more global, schematic impressions. Moreover, children who are in classrooms where factual answers are emphasized often get little opportunity to use oral language to elaborate their ideas or to talk in-depth about meaningful content; they too often spend their time answering factual questions in monosyllables, or filling in blanks on worksheets in the same, uninspired manner.

# CHAPTER 1

# THE QUESTION OF QUESTIONS

Most educators agree that one of the major goals of teaching is to help children learn to make reasoned decisions in life. To do so children must be taught to actively solve problems, to think critically and creatively, and to feel good about themselves. They acquire these necessary thinking skills by learning to form and respond to critical questions. Teachers may help children accomplish these goals within a required curriculum of knowledge acquisition, or, in sharp contrast, they may simply fill the minds of children with a series of unrelated facts as if they were empty vessels.

Learning to ask appropriate questions is a sophisticated art form, but it's an area that receives short shrift in most teacher education programs. This is unfortunate because research indicates that teachers specifically trained to ask high-quality questions show significant improvement in constructing and using such questions in the classroom (Angletti 1991) and so become more adept at stimulating the human potential of their students. As well, being aware of the classification of questions and their myriad forms helps teachers determine just how well they are doing at engaging their students in critical and creative thinking levels.

Questioning is effective for so many purposes that teachers must be skilled in its use. They need to know the many ways of asking and how to adapt the type and form of each question to the purpose for which it is asked. Because questioning is so important, this entire chapter is devoted to helping the teacher become familiar with the different levels of questions in both the cognitive and the affective domains.

## TYPES OF QUESTIONS

### THE COGNITIVE DOMAIN

The basic framework for the types of questions used in most classrooms comes from the work of Benjamin Bloom. In his book *Taxonomy of Educational Objectives,* Bloom (1984) presents six major cognitive—or thinking—operations: knowledge, comprehension, application, analysis, synthesis, and evaluation (see figure 1).

Bloom's six types of questions can be grouped into three larger categories according to the level of processing that is required of students who are answering them. Level I questions—"knowledge" and "comprehension"—are lower-level questions; they require children to gather and recall data, but call for little complex thinking. They are designed mainly to solicit concepts, information, feelings, or experiences from students, which have been gathered in the past and stored in the memory. Level II questions—"application" and "analysis"—ask the students to begin to process data and to integrate new content with their own experiences. Level III questions—"synthesis" and "evaluation"— are called higher-level questions; they require a high level of mental operation. To answer, the students must engage in more abstract and sophisticated thinking that requires them to evaluate data in an entirely new situation, or to predict future events. At this level, questions are designed to encourage students to think intuitively, creatively, and hypothetically, to use their imaginations, to reveal their value systems, or to make judgments.

### THE AFFECTIVE DOMAIN

Bloom also considered questions in the affective domain that deal mainly with feelings and emotion. In reality, the cognitive and affective domains cannot be divided, for it is almost impossible for children—or anyone—to process information without some emotional response. Nor can they actually *value* an issue without having thought about it. It seems that both domains tend to blend and flow concurrently. However, certain questions may be more relevant to one domain than to the other.

| Level | Question Type | Response Behaviors | Eliciting Question Starters |
|-------|---------------|--------------------|-----------------------------|
| I | Knowledge | Recalling facts or observation. Recalling definitions. | 1. Who...? 2. What...? 3. Where...? 4. When...? 5. Define (the word *prosper*) |
| | Comprehension | Giving descriptions. | 1. Describe (what happened when the third goat went over the bridge)? 2. What is the main idea (in this paragraph)? 3. How are (these two fruits alike)? |
| II | Application | Applying techniques. | 1. If...then... 2. What is (the perimeter of your living room)? |
| | Analysis | Identifying motives or causes. Making inferences. Finding evidence to support generalizations. | 1. Why (did Old Yeller die)? 2. Now that we've studied whales, what can we conclude about zoos? (assumptions) 3. What evidence can you find to support (the point of view that students should not receive grades)? |
| III | Synthesis | Solving problems. Making predictions. Producing original communications. | 1. Can you think up (a way to test this)? 2. How can we solve (this problem)? 3. How can we improve (our research)? 4. What will happen (now that we've found a cure for cancer)? 5. What do you predict would happen (if we all looked the same)? |
| | Evaluation | Giving opinions about issues. Judging the validity of ideas. Judging the merit of problem solutions. Judging the quality of art and other products. Justifying opinions and ideas. | 1. Do you agree (with José)? 2. Do you believe (that this is the best way to proceed)? Why? 3. Do you think (that it is right to judge criminals)? Why? 4. What is your opinion (on this matter)? Why? 5. Would it be better (to do it this way)? Why? 6. Which (video) did you like? Why? |

*Figure 1. Cognitive Domain: Questioning Strategies*

The five types of questions in the affective domain are: receiving, responding, valuing, organization, and characterization. These can be grouped according to the level of processing required, as are the cognitive domain questions. "Receiving" and "responding" are considered Level I, or lower-level questions. While both require that a child be somewhat involved in the activity or idea, there is little real commitment in his answer. Level II questions are "valuing" questions and require students to "think harder" and thus to commit themselves to the degree that the resulting behavior is consistent and stable enough to be called a belief or an attitude. Level III questions, or higher-level questions, involve "organization" and "characterization." Such questions are successful when they provoke the students to internalize their values, act upon those values, or organize them into a consistent value system that they are willing to defend.

Affective-type questions representing all levels should be present in all class discussions, although not all levels need to be used in any particular lesson. Just as the skilled teacher devises cognitive questions to stimulate students to process information with the final goal of analyzing data and evaluating it, the teacher using affective questions wishes to elicit feeling-laden responses from students, and invites them to care and develop a value system that will become part of their daily lives. Figure 2 provides a description of the categories of questions in the affective domain.

## OTHER TYPES OF QUESTIONS

In addition to Bloom's two taxonomies, Costa (1991) identifies several other ways of looking at the questions teachers ask in classrooms to elicit desired responses: clarifying, cuing, focus, and probing.

+ *Clarifying questions.* When the teacher is not certain she understands what the student is saying, or when the teacher hopes to get the student to elaborate, a helpful question is asked, such as: "Are you saying that gang members provide the same function as parents? Would you tell us more about why you think that is so?"

| Level | Question Type | Response Behaviors | Eliciting Question Starters |
|---|---|---|---|
| I | Receiving (attending) | Awareness of environment. Willingness to receive. | 1. Which would you prefer…? 2. Identify the person who… 3. Listen to these CDs… 4. Are you aware that…? |
| | Responding | Acquiescence in responding. Willingness to respond. Satisfaction in response. | 1. Do you like to sing? 2. Did you observe the difference between the two pieces? 3. Are you willing to go to the ballet? |
| II | Valuing | Acceptance of a value. Preference for a value. Commitment. | 1. Defend your stance (on gun control). 2. Do you feel (responsible for the homeless)? 3. Rank order your preferences… 4. Do you agree or disagree that…? |
| III | Organization | Conceptualization of a value. Organization of a value system. | 1. In your opinion (is this money well spent)? 2. As you view (the war, should we have entered the conflict)? 3. In your own words, explain the issue. 4. Have you weighed the alternatives (for not using animal research)? |
| | Characterization | Generalized set. A philosophy of life. Values are internalized. | 1. What will you do (about pollution)? 2. Are you willing to (give up lunch one day a week for the homeless)? 3. What is your philosophy (on mercy killings)? 4. Which of the following beliefs would you say is the most important in your life? |

*Figure 2. Affective Domain: Questioning Strategies*

or "Is there more you could say about why you feel the boy was just asking for trouble by entering the contest?"

+ *Cuing questions.* Often a teacher asks a leading question to launch a lesson only to be greeted by total silence, because the students lack the background information to answer the question. In these instances, the teacher provides *hints* in the form of questions. For example, the teacher might ask "Why do you think so many people went westward in the pioneer days?" When greeted with silence, the teacher tries cuing: "What effect did the discovery of gold in California have on the settlers' decision to go West?" or "What discovery in California caused great excitement?"

+ *Focus questions.* A teacher asks a focus question when directing the learners' attention to a particular issue. For example, a teacher might ask "Should there be a leash law in Sacramento?" to focus student attention on the topic. Then she can begin to elicit opinions and draw the whole class into a discussion on the pros and cons of the issue.

+ *Probing questions.* Without the follow-up of probing questions many important questions receive simple responses. For example, the teacher asks, "Should we have sent troops to Somalia?" and Hoa answers, "Absolutely not!" The teacher has an answer to the critical question, but no reasoned decision. "Why do you think that, Hoa?" the teacher probes, and soon discovers the depth of the child's thinking on the subject.

## THE PERVASIVE IRE

A final word about questions concerns not the *design* of the questions themselves, but how the responses are evaluated by the questioner. For critical and creative thinking to flourish in a classroom, children must be free to respond to questions from their own trajectory of experience, attitudes, and values. Unfortunately, in most classrooms, discussions follow the time-honored Initiate-Respond-Evaluate (IRE) pattern of question and answer (Roller 1989). For instance, using this pattern, the teacher asks a question designed to get children ready to interact with what they are about to read. She tries to connect what the students already know about a subject so that they will be more likely to assimilate new information easily. For example, prior to reading a story about a youngster who has won a prestigious award, the teacher initiates discussion by asking if anyone in the class has ever won an award. A child responds by saying her father once won an award in a refugee camp, for touching his nose with his tongue. Very quickly, almost subconsciously, the teacher evaluates and decides the response does not meet her expectation; it is not the academic-type award she has in mind. The child who answered the question has been unintentionally rebuked. From this she learns that she must try to figure out the answer that the teacher has in mind. Or perhaps she learns that it is safer to not respond at all (Cecil 1990). Teachers who use IRE have a *hidden agenda* in asking the question and therefore control the interchange, subtly insisting that all learners must match their level of language, experience, and values. These teachers may, in fact, continue to ask children for responses to a particular question until they get the answer they want.

## USING THE TAXONOMY OF QUESTIONS

The taxonomy of questions just explored offers a variety of interesting possibilities related to teaching and learning. These possibilities will be presented in random order, as individual differences in teachers and classrooms of children have a significant influence on the usability and success of a particular approach to questioning techniques. The following are ways in which awareness of types of questions could impact various curricular components:

+ *Building questions from reading material.* Knowing the breadth of possibilities in both the cognitive and affective domains helps teachers create questions that build on one another hierarchically. Also, awareness of several models, descriptions, and verb delineations helps teachers develop questions that focus on particular cognitive skills or affective responses (see figure 3, page 15).

+ *Selecting curriculum.* When selecting different learning activities across the spectrum of the curriculum, the overall objectives can be tied to reinforcing particular thinking skills or affective responses.

This criterion for selection allows the teacher, as key decision maker, to choose activities that have clear, broad-based instructional goals.

✦ *Purchasing instructional materials.* The taxonomy of questions could be used as a guideline to evaluate whether instructional material taps the full range of thinking and valuing levels, as opposed to whether or not specific content matter is covered.

✦ *Teaching the taxonomy to students.* Children can be taught to use the taxonomy by having them select from a series of options that cover the entire range of thinking processes. To do this, they would first choose an issue, theme, or problem. Then, using question types, they would select verbs from each level of the taxonomy as a way to explore the topic (see figure 3). Finally, from the top rung of either the cognitive or affective taxonomy, they would select a means for displaying a product of their exploration. In the affective domain, for example, an exploration of capital punishment might lead to a final product of a letter to the child's government representative stating the student's argument for or against. In the cognitive domain, an essay might be the vehicle through which a child evaluates the relative validity of passive resistance by exploring the life of Mahatma Gandhi or Martin Luther King, Jr.

✦ *Independent study.* Many teachers are uncomfortable with independent study by learners because they must evaluate an *orphan* product; it cannot be measured against twenty-nine others that help establish a norm. But in independent study, higher-level thinking skills are experienced by the learner in a natural way. Using the taxonomy as a criterion, the teacher can analyze the range of thinking (or valuing) within the student's activities.

✦ *Assessing verbal interactions.* Teachers know intuitively that classroom discussion provides a meaningful forum for oral language development, intellectual experiences, and a chance to discover values; however, evaluating such discussion may be difficult in this age of accountability. Informally, the quality and type of questions initiated by each student can be recorded—teachers could use this

| | | |
|---|---|---|
| **Name** | **Date** | |
| **Theme** | **Martin Luther King, Jr.: The Life of a Great Man** | |

**Question Type 1.** Choose from the following verbs:

| | | |
|---|---|---|
| define | describe | observe |
| list | match | notice |
| identify | locate | |

*Student:* I will describe the early life of Martin Luther King, Jr.

**Question Type 2.** Choose from the following verbs:

| | | |
|---|---|---|
| explain | rewrite | summarize |
| convert | interpret | give examples |
| paraphrase | respond | |

*Student:* I will paraphrase Martin Luther King, Jr.'s "I Have a Dream" speech.

**Question Type 3.** Choose from the following verbs:

| | | |
|---|---|---|
| demonstrate | show | support an opinion |
| construct | operate | apply |

*Student:* I will support my opinion that Dr. King was a "Great Man" by showing the many ways he changed life for Black Americans.

**Question Type 4.** Choose from the following verbs:

| | | |
|---|---|---|
| organize | deduct | value |
| infer | compare | analyze |
| contrast | categorize | distinguish |

*Student:* I will compare the life of Dr. Martin Luther King, Jr. to that of Mahatma Gandhi.

**Question Type 5.** Choose from the following verbs:

| | | | |
|---|---|---|---|
| create | design | suppose | compose |
| support | rearrange | combine | |

*Student:* I will create my own "I Have a Dream" speech, including all the goals Dr. King had that have not yet been realized.

**Question Type 6.** Choose from the following verbs:

| | | | |
|---|---|---|---|
| judge | debate | characterize | support |
| appraise | criticize | evaluate | |

*Student:* I will write an essay in support of passive resistance and how it could end the violence in North American cities.

*Figure 3. Teaching the taxonomy to students*

taxonomy as a means of measuring student verbal interactions at differing intervals during the school year. Such informal anecdotal information fits in well with the use of portfolios and authentic assessment.

The above suggestions represent several possible uses for the cognitive and affective questioning taxonomies. While their usefulness will vary according to different teaching styles and situations, they do provide some help: structure and a viable rationale for the curriculum selection process. If used appropriately and integrated throughout the curriculum, the taxonomies and other types of questions can offer welcome guidelines for the teacher wishing to boost the level of cognitive and affective functioning in the classroom.

## AN EXERCISE FOR IDENTIFYING TYPES AND LEVELS OF QUESTIONS

The exercise that follows (see figure 4) is designed to assess your recognition and understanding of the types (cognitive or affective) and levels (I, II, or III) of questions that have been discussed in this chapter. Mark each of the questions with a letter (*C* for cognitive or *A* for affective) and a number corresponding to the level (I, II, or III). In many cases, a question can contain elements of both domains or, depending on the actual response, straddle two different levels. For this exercise, however, mark the type and level that best fits the question.

## An Exercise for Identifying Types and Levels of Questions

_____ 1. Do you recall the difference between a camel and a dromedary?

_____ 2. What is your reaction to the position Mr. Potter has taken regarding the leash law in Sacramento?

_____ 3. Explain how the habitats of the two turtles are similar. How are they different?

_____ 4. Which of the poems do you think was the most interesting?

_____ 5. If you were offered a trip to China this summer, how would you react?

_____ 6. Compose an essay that would tell about your outlook on school.

_____ 7. What is the capital of Illinois?

_____ 8. Indicate your reaction to the man who says he loves nature but who goes deer hunting.

_____ 9. How do you feel about reading?

_____ 10. How might these geometric shapes be grouped?

_____ 11. What do you think will happen when Jud finds out that the boy has Shiloh?

_____ 12. How does life today differ from life in the times of the pioneers?

_____ 13. Write a short essay relating how you interpret the role of government with regard to providing housing for the homeless.

_____ 14. Indicate philosophically how you feel about the death penalty.

_____ 15. What do you think transportation will be like in the year 2525?

_____ 16. What do you think will be the long-term effect of pollution if nothing is done to stop it?

_____ 17. Did the position Dan Quayle, former vice president of the United States, take on the family make you want to like him? Why or why not?

_____ 18. What do you think caused Jesse to change his mind about Leslie?

_____ 19. Do all trees have leaves?

_____ 20. Is there any type of activity you would like to try over any other?

**Answers:**

13. C,II  14. A,III  15. C,III  16. C,III  17. A,II  18. C,II  19. C,II  20. A,II

1. C,I  2. A,II  3. C,I  4. A,I  5. A,II  6. C,III  7. C,I  8. A,II  9. A,I  10. C,II  11. C,III  12. C,II

*Figure 4. Assessment Exercise*

# CHAPTER 2

# THE IDEAL CLIMATE
# FOR QUESTIONING

The climate in many classrooms in North America inhibits children from asking and answering questions. In such classrooms, silence and order are the most important features and strict adherence to teacher-imposed rules are dutifully enforced. The atmosphere can be described as chilly, and the brains of learners have great difficulty warming up. Children's spirits shrink and their little bodies droop. Their minds don't grow; they contract. Children feel self-conscious about expressing themselves and are therefore never totally engaged in learning.

Fortunately, there are also many classroom in North America in which children's faces are alive with excitement and every hand is up because every child's imagination is churning and producing ideas. Young minds are being stimulated and challenged. The moment an observer enters the classroom, that person notices how questions and answers abound, often initiated by the children themselves. Classrooms that reflect this kind of enthusiastic intellectual interchange strengthen the spirit of children and spark the flames of curiosity and self-worth. In these classrooms, children are proud of their work, respect their own ideas and the ideas of others, and welcome new experiences. Such classrooms reflect Sylvia Ashton-Warner's observation that "energy and curiosity make good deskmates" (1974: 117).

· · · ·

In this chapter we examine the classroom filled with enthusiasm, the kind that is most conducive to encouraging children to ask and answer questions reflectively and honestly. We also explore common practices to avoid because they tend to squelch open and thoughtful behavior.

## REMOVING BLOCKS TO CRITICAL THINKING

One way to develop the willingness and the ability to ask and answer critical and creative questions is to remove factors that block the free flow of the production of ideas. In some cases, the teacher must try to undo patterns of passive behavior that have been established in previous teacher-dominated classrooms; in other cases, the teacher may need to provide children with a necessary knowledge base from which they can begin to ask and answer reflective questions.

### KNOWLEDGE

For children to ask and answer reflective questions, they must have some basis of factual awareness of the topic or problem under investigation; in other words, they cannot examine the topic critically or offer creative solutions or observations if they know nothing about the subject. For example, a teacher may launch a unit on the rain forest with the high-level, critical-thinking question, "Why are rain forests important to us?" While this may be a good question, it is a poor *first* question, for it is possible that many children do not know enough about the issues inherent in the question to offer a wide range of cogent responses. By contrast, after defining rain forests and researching the effects of forests on our oxygen supply, exploring how wood is used in our daily lives, and discussing the pros and cons of deforestation, children are much more able and eager to respond to the original question, backing up their ideas, beliefs, and opinions with facts. Many skills are required before thoughtful, reasoned questions can be asked and answered, but acquiring the necessary knowledge base is an important first step in the total process.

### HABITS

Habit is another block to a free flow of questions and answers in the classroom. Certainly, it is human nature to get *comfortable* with a particular way of doing things, and the same is true with the asking and answering of questions. An example of this is when teachers ask *all* the questions (especially as indicated in the teacher's manual), instead of allowing children to ask their *own* questions and to answer one another's questions. While teachers may support the idea of a child-centered classroom in theory, many find themselves unable to break the habit of being the one controlling the discussion.

Another habit common to teachers is same-line questioning, used in the same way, to all groups of learners, without considering the size of the group, the ability levels, the language proficiency, and so on. Even without considering the unique qualities of the group, it is still true that a variety of question-and-answer techniques enhance the intellectual climate of the classroom. Teachers should take a long, hard look at their classrooms to determine if they need to free themselves from entrenched questioning habits.

Young children, too, develop habits that are hard to break. Due to a variety of cultural and personality factors, they may establish passive stances and they often require special encouragement by a caring teacher to change from passive listeners to active participants in question-and-answer exchanges.

## ATTITUDES

The final block to a free flow production of questions and answers in the classroom are the attitudes of both teachers and learners that can develop over time. A terse, negative response such as, "*That* will never work!" to any new idea (for example, a change away from a teacher-centered classroom toward a child-centered classroom) or an abrupt move to asking very young children high-level questions rather than just factual ones is counterproductive. Teachers must actively attempt to alter these negative attitudes so that "It can't work!" becomes "Maybe I'll try and see!"

Authority—who is in charge—is another problem. Teachers who see themselves as the ultimate authority in their classrooms often have a difficult time dealing with open-ended questions for which they may not have all the answers. Nor are they comfortable allowing students to lead the discussion.

Teachers must also concern themselves with learners' attitudes toward authority. Many children are passive in the classroom, expect the teacher to have all the answers, and feel confused when they are asked to offer a viewpoint that may differ from the teacher's. Such children need to be invited to initiate questions concerning their own interests in the more accepting atmosphere of a student-centered classroom.

## FACILITATING THE FREE FLOW OF PRODUCTION

As we have discussed, the teacher's goal is to help the students learn how to solve problems, make decisions, think critically and creatively, and feel good about themselves and their learning. How the teacher constructs questions and carries out questioning strategies has everything to do with the realization of these goals. In the remainder of this chapter we look at how to prepare and implement the kinds of questions that arouse student interest and encourage their participation.

### CAREFUL PLANNING OF QUESTIONS

Thorough preparation helps ensure that questions are clear and specific to children, that the vocabulary is appropriate for the targeted learners, and that each question matches its purpose. Questions should be incorporated into all lessons as effective instructional devices, welcomed pauses for reflection, attention grabbers, and as viable checks for student comprehension.

For units and learning centers, one driving investigative question should be created to connect all the activities into a meaningful whole. For example, the question, "Why did the pioneers go westward?" allows the teacher and students to focus on answering this one pivotal question throughout the rest of the unit. With a clear focus in mind, teachers are less likely to include frivolous activities about pioneers—activities that may be fun for the children but do not add significantly to the body of knowledge being developed. Similarly, if students are aware of the overall investigative question, their responses to oral and written questions are much more likely to remain focused on the topic and they can more easily understand how the activity is connected to other activities in the unit or learning center.

Additionally, when planning open-ended critical or creative questions, teachers must guard against having in mind preconceived answers that reflect their personal world view, values, and/or culture. They can best accomplish this by asking themselves, "Do I have an answer for this question already in mind? Does it reflect my personal belief system? Will I be open to a variety of thoughtful answers that do *not* match the ones that I have developed?"

## MATCHING QUESTIONS WITH THEIR PURPOSES

Carefully planned questions can be sequenced and worded to match the appropriate level of cognitive and affective thinking that the teacher desires of the students. To help students develop more effective thinking skills, the teacher must create questions that are easily understood and that students can relate to their own experiences. Constant modeling

| Specific Question | Vague Question |
|---|---|
| ✦ What evidence do you have to support your ideas about that? | ✦ How do you know that? |
| ✦ What does that music remind you of in your own life? | ✦ Do you like that music? |
| ✦ How would you apply that concept to your own budgeting? | ✦ What did you learn about budgeting? |
| ✦ Could you explain how these two elephants differ? | ✦ What do you think about these two elephants? |

*Figure 5. Question Comparison: Specific vs. Vague*

of the appropriate cognitive or affective terminology helps students focus their thinking in specific ways. Figure 5 (see page 23) provides examples of good, specifically-worded questions in one column and poor, vaguely-worded questions in the other.

## CONDUCTING "GRAND CONVERSATIONS"

To involve children in thinking, feeling, and responding to ideas, issues, events, and characters in a book, teachers must focus on questioning strategies that resemble "grand conversations" rather than the more common *gentle inquisitions* (Bird 1988; Edelsky 1988). Grand conversations enable students to express their ideas honestly and to share their thoughts and experiences with their classmates in a meaningful way. Grand conversations are most similar to the lively discussions that occur in adult book groups; that is, the focus is on the relevance and personal reactions of the participants; every member is invited to participate.

During gentle inquisitions, on the other hand, the tone of the classroom interaction is usually one of checking up on the students to see if they have read the book. The teacher dutifully asks the questions and the students dutifully answer them; then the teacher decides if the students have understood. While there is certainly a need for diagnosing student comprehension, studies have shown that an inordinate amount of time is spent in this kind of robotic assessment in lieu of richer literary discussions (Wendler, Samuels & Moore 1989), and at the expense of time spent on critical thinking (Langer, Applebee, Mullis & Foertsch 1990).

## STUDENT-DIRECTED DISCUSSIONS

One of the most detrimental behaviors to the critical and creative thinking of youngsters is when teachers dominate all the talk in a classroom. Uncomfortable with silence, or a pace perceived to be *plodding,* the teacher asks one question after another and adds extraneous information to the children's responses, thus confusing the students and allowing them little time to think or connect ideas. By contrast, in a student-centered classroom, the teacher becomes *the guide on the side,* rather than the *sage on the stage*—a true facilitator rather than the *guru* with all the answers. In such a classroom, a child may ask a question that another child will respond to. A third child may politely challenge the response or add additional perspective while the teacher merely affirms and praises all the participants. For example:

RENÉ: Why do camels have humps?

TEACHER: Does anyone have any idea about that?

RAÚL: I think I read that they store food and water in their humps.

GRACIELA: I think you are right, but some camels only have one hump. They must be the kind that have not far to go in the desert.

RAÚL: No, I think they're just a different breed, like cats that can have long furry tails, or Manxes that have no tails.

TEACHER: You have raised some interesting questions. Why don't you look up *camel* in the encyclopedia and see what you can find out? Then get back to us.

## WAIT TIME

Critical and creative thinking and reflection take time. Unfortunately, it is often the children who think the most quickly or are the most vociferous who are provided practice and exercise in these important skills. These students rapidly establish a pattern in the classroom: The teacher asks a thought-provoking question and the six "eager beavers" quickly and exuberantly have their hands up with an answer. The other children have not even had a chance to consider the question; moreover, they decide that if they delay raising their hands they will not be accountable for thinking about and answering the questions. The quick-thinking few answer the majority of the questions, delighting the teacher with their ability to keep up a snappy pace, while the others sit passively by.

For critical and creative questions to be produced and responded to by *every* learner, each child must be given time to consider the question. The teacher must invite the opinions and ideas of even the most reticent child and let it be known that everyone will have a chance to respond.

After asking a question, a general rule is to wait at least three seconds and as long as ten to offer *all* children the opportunity to think. Though this may seem like a brief period of time, stop reading, look at a watch or clock, and observe how long three seconds is and then ten seconds. Because most of us are not accustomed to silence in a classroom, even three seconds can seem like an eternity. If for some reason only a few students have their hands up after three to ten seconds of wait time, ask the question again and make eye contact with some learners who do not have their hands up (but do not reword a carefully crafted question or students are apt to perceive it as a new question). Again, pause for several seconds; then, if most learners have still not raised their hands, call on a student who has his hand up, and then another, allowing more wait time for the children who may still be thinking. Soon you will get responses that other children can build upon. You should never have to answer your own questions.

## EQUALITY IN THE CLASSROOM

When you ask questions, do not recognize students who randomly shout out responses; instead, insist that they raise their hands and wait to be called upon before they respond. Though many teachers worry that such rules are unnecessarily rigid and other teachers are delighted when they hear immediate responses shouted out, such behavior results in unequal interactions. Boys tend to be more vociferous than girls in class, for example. Even at the college level, males are more vocal than their female counterparts, and when allowed by the professor, dominate and interrupt their female peers. On the other hand, children from certain cultural groups, such as the Vietnamese, are taught at home to be polite and even self-effacing; they, too, are usually overshadowed by children choosing to shout out answers (Davidman

1994). Therefore, every teacher should discourage students from shouting out answers, thereby ensuring more equal distribution of interaction time in the classroom.

A related issue is the tendency of teachers to call on the brighter students and allowing them more time to articulate their responses. A teacher who waits for less time when calling on a slower student, or students of one gender more than the other, is showing a bias or a lack of confidence in certain students—both detrimental in the effort to establish for *all* students a positive, equal, and safe environment for classroom learning. It is critical that teachers show confidence in all students and not discriminate between them.

Most teachers are committed to providing fair treatment to all their learners, but are simply unaware of many seemingly discriminatory practices. To provide egalitarian instruction takes concentration and effort. But it is possible. Teachers can prepare a seating chart on a clipboard and make a mark next to the student's name as each is called upon. Also, teachers can practice giving equal wait time to all learners (place one hand behind your back and slowly fold back your fingers one at a time, with each finger folded representing one second of wait time). Finally, an invited observer or a videotape of a lesson can allow a teacher the luxury of being able to focus on the fairness of the distribution of responses in her classroom.

## APPROPRIATE USE OF PRAISE

The use of strong praise is sometimes appropriate—when working with very young children, second-language learners who are just emerging from the *silent period* (the period during which they are first silent as they develop receptive language), children with special needs, or when asking questions of factual or low-level recall, such as "Jeff, what was the falcon's name?" But when the goal is to have the students think critically and creatively, the teacher should be more careful with the use of strong praise for student responses, as it tends to squelch higher-level thinking.

Instead, the goal should be to help children find intrinsic sources for their own motivation. Strong praise tends to encourage conformity, causing children to depend on the praise giver for their worth, rather than on themselves and their own satisfaction with their ideas. A strong praise (active acceptance) response is exemplified by a teacher who responds to a child's answer with, "That's exactly right! Excellent job!" On the other hand, passive acceptance responses, such as "Yes, that is one way to think about Kay's problem," keep the window open for further thinking on the part of others in the class.

Another example of a passive acceptance response is one used in brainstorming sessions when the teacher says, "After asking the question and giving you some time to think about it, I would like to hear everyone's ideas and I will write them on the chalkboard." Only after all the students' responses have been recorded does the class begin its consideration of each individual response. In the classroom, that kind of nonjudgmental acceptance of all ideas generates the greatest amount of critical and creative reflection.

## CONTINUALLY ENCOURAGING INQUIRY

We derive meaning and knowledge by asking questions. The ability to recognize problems and form questions is a skill—and the key to problem solving and the development of critical-thinking skills. It is the responsibility of teachers to encourage children to formulate questions and to help them word their questions so that possible answers can be sought—and found. This process is necessary to build a base of knowledge that can be called upon again and again as a way to connect, interpret, and assimilate new information in new situations.

Through constant practice in the use of questioning, students soon discover that inquiry is the cornerstone to critical thinking and real-world problem solving, and that there are usually no absolute answers. Some answers are better than others, not *correct* or *incorrect.* The student must be taught to (1) recognize the problem; (2) formulate a question about the problem (Should I take ballet lessons or piano lessons? Should I sign up for soccer or get a paper route? Should

I drink orange juice or a Coke?); (3) collect all the necessary data; and (4) arrive at a temporarily acceptable answer to the problem, while understanding that at some later time new data may call for modification of the conclusion.

Finally, students can be encouraged to ask questions about everything and anything by being told there is no such thing as a "dumb question." For instance, students (like everyone else) may ask questions that seem out of context with the content of a particular lesson or for which they could just as easily look up the answers themselves. Such questions consume precious class time, and, understandably, can frustrate the teacher. A teacher's initial reaction might be to quickly brush off the question or to tell the student to look up the answer, or to "stay on the subject." Such reactions, however, can have a negative effect on the openness of the entire class. Instead of showing irritation, the teacher should answer kindly and professionally, and later try to zero in on the youngster's purpose for asking such a question. Often a seemingly off-the-mark question signals a child's need for recognition and more interaction with the teacher. If this is the case, a possible response might be "You asked an interesting question and I would like to discuss it with you. Could we meet together before or after school, or at recess, to talk?"

Student questions can and should be used as springboards for further questions, investigations, and discussions. Students should be encouraged to ask the entire spectrum of questions—questions that politely challenge the textbook, current practices, and other person's statements (including the teacher's)—and to seek the facts or evidence behind a statement, practice, or policy.

## ADMITTING LACK OF KNOWLEDGE

Nothing diminishes a teacher's credibility more than the students' realization she has *bluffed* an answer to a question. Children, especially very young ones, tend to believe their teacher knows *everything*—more, even, than their parents. This is a tremendous burden for even the most well-informed teacher, for no one, of course, knows everything. It is important, therefore, to admit it when you do not know the answer to a question. Admitting you do not know everything allows students to see you are human; it also gives children—regardless of their ability—permission to not know all the answers, without damaging their self-esteem. But it is important to demonstrate you care about the question, you know where and how to find possible answers to the question, and you are willing to help students develop these same skills.

## A CHECKLIST FOR CLASSROOM CLIMATE

Use the following questions as a checklist to determine if the atmosphere in your classroom is conducive to the free flow of questions and answers. Most of the questions relate to the activities presented in this book. The list is not exhaustive, but hopefully, will encourage you to generate other reflective questions to help you discover if you are creating a climate necessary for children to become deeply involved with questions.

+ Am I providing an atmosphere that is nonthreatening and that encourages all students to articulate the questions they really want to ask?

+ Am I providing plenty of opportunities for children to discuss their ideas with their classmates and with me?

+ Am I providing enough factual information first so that students have foundations for discussion?

+ Am I offering specific suggestions to students about how to plan, organize, and implement particular question strategies for processing information?

+ Do I schedule opportunities for children to react cognitively and affectively to questions encountered or planned?

+ Do I plan questioning sessions so that my questions are clear and my vocabulary is appropriate to my learners?

- Do I avoid dominating the discussions?
- Do I provide enough wait time so that all children have an opportunity to carefully consider the questions?
- Do I provide an equal opportunity for all learners to answer questions and participate in discussions?
- Do I, as the teacher, model good questioning?
- Am I open to new ways of organizing my classroom and doing things?
- Am I willing to admit that I don't have all the answers and can I show children how to discover the answers to questions?

. . . .

# SUMMARY OF PART I

Asking good questions is essential when receiving and delivering information and ideas. In chapter 1, we explored the kinds of questions that are possible. We did this through the two taxonomies proposed by Benjamin Bloom, and described each level of questioning and example questions for each level. The cognitive domain is considered the basic framework for all classroom questioning; the affective domain provides a complementary structure for many feelings, emotions, and values that are integral to learning.

We also explored other types of questions that teachers ask for a variety of purposes. Teachers ask *clarifying questions* to understand what a child is really trying to say, *cuing questions* to give hints, *focus questions* to direct the attention of learners, and *probing questions* to encourage children to elaborate beyond single-word responses. A caveat was issued regarding the practice of Initiate-Respond-Evaluate, which is prevalent in many elementary classrooms. While the level of critical discussion emanating from the use of IRE may be high, the danger comes when the teacher has already decided upon the answers to the questions. If a child's answer differs from the teacher's, or if the child is unable to match the teacher's cultural references, the child will not succeed in such a forum. Often teachers are not fully aware of their own IRE tactics. An excellent way to self-assess is to make videos of class discussions.

Some suggestions were also offered in this chapter as to how the taxonomies of questions could be put to use in a variety of classroom situations.

Finally, a short quiz gave you a way to see if you are able to discriminate between the two domains of questioning, and if you can recognize what level of mental processing would be at work if such questions were asked.

Asking children the *right* questions so they will be fully involved in processing and applying knowledge and ideas may not be educational salvation, but it is certainly a step in the right direction. Yamomoto (1969: 61) once mused "Each tree is known by its own fruit...and we cannot expect to gather figs from thorns or grapes from a bramble bush." Similarly, if we place a premium on only low-level, factual questions, we are then settling for the creation of passive learners. If, on the other hand, we involve children in answering critical and creative questions, and we prod them to carefully formulate their attitudes and beliefs, we contribute to their competence and support their search for their own human identity.

For children to feel safe and comfortable enough to enter into classroom discussions where there is a free flow of questions and answers, the classroom climate must be conducive to lively interchange. In chapter 2, we explored a panoply of considerations for creating such a classroom.

The key factor in maintaining a positive atmosphere that fosters the free flow of questions and answers is *freedom*. It means that children are free to raise a wide range of questions, and free to pose questions that interest them. It means that the teacher accepts children's feelings, beliefs, and occasionally, an off-the-mark question. It also means the teacher listens carefully to children and is enthusiastic in working with them so they process their questions. This *free* atmosphere may be structured in other ways, but it is always one where the teacher and other children welcome and respect one another's ideas.

Finally, a free atmosphere for questioning is one in which the teacher and students demonstrate that they have confidence in each other. The teacher has enough confidence in the students to allow many discussions to be student-centered, and the children have enough confidence in the teacher that they participate fully in such discussions.

However, the teacher and students are both confident enough to admit they don't know *all* the answers to *all* the questions, but joyfully share in the knowledge gained in their discoveries. In such a classroom, there is no such thing as a dumb question, but the level of questions asked rises dramatically as the exemplar of good questioning in this classroom—the teacher—continually stimulates the critical and creative thinking of each and every child.

# PART II

# QUESTIONING STRATEGIES

The *question* is a pivotal—if not *the* pivotal—component in critical thinking. Whether you are functioning at a thinking or at a feeling level with data, you need to generate well-constructed questions. And the questions you create and the manner in which you phrase and sequence them strongly influence the quality, significance, and accuracy of the learners' conclusions and what is done with those conclusions.

Becoming adept at asking questions is an important but deceptively difficult skill to learn. Uncovering the many dimensions of inquiry, the numerous questioning strategies, and your role in them take time and practice. But it is time well spent, for it provides students access to experiences with critical thinking that they can use for the rest of their lives.

Since the question is the linchpin to meaningful engagement with learning, teachers need to be good questioners and be able to provide students with formal and informal situations in which they can learn about the realm of questions and questioning.

· · · ·

One rich source for questions is often overlooked—the students. Lee Galda and his associates (1993) assert that all discussions should be student-centered, giving *all* children the opportunity to freely express their thoughts and opinions. In reality, teachers do most of the talking and questioning. This is unfortunate. Carin and Sund (1991) find students attain significantly higher levels of thinking when they are encouraged to develop skill in generating critical and creative questions and when they are provided opportunities for dialogue with classmates about the questions posed and conclusions derived from information they encounter.

Catherine Cornbleth (1975) presents some compelling evidence to support student questioning:

+ All students can be encouraged to ask productive or critical questions.
+ The more questions a student asks in any one time period, the greater the probability that the questions will be higher level.
+ Students become more actively engaged in classes where they are encouraged to ask their own questions.

Nor should student *self*-questioning be overlooked as a viable strategy. Self-questioning strategies teach children to ask their own questions as they read. Mason and Au (1986: 157) explore the value of self-questioning:

> To be able to ask questions, students must be actively thinking about and working with the text. In asking their own pre-questions, that is, questions about material not yet read, students decide what the selections might be about and what they might want to learn from it. This gives students a chance to set their own purposes for reading.

Clearly, self-questioning can enhance comprehension both by encouraging active involvement and by giving children authentic experiences in setting their own purposes for reading. Finally, teaching children to construct their own questions can greatly improve retention of both narrative and expository material (Singer & Donlon 1982; Balajthy 1983).

In the following chapters, I present a series of teacher-tested questioning strategies. In chapters 3 and 4, I respond to the query, "How can I model good questioning strategies that will help my students think more critically?" It is important to understand the basic reason for each strategy and have a general idea of how that strategy is used in the context of a lesson in a real classroom. To this end, I provide a selection of exemplary strategies that you can use to model effective questions. These have been designed to show children how to develop conceptual frameworks for thinking critically in both the affective and cognitive domains.

In chapters 5 and 6, I explore several strategies that you can use to promote self-questioning strategies in your students. The goals of each strategy are to help children think more critically and creatively while reading, and to help them become more proficient at setting appropriate purposes and expectations for reading. Any of these strategies can be used as a refreshing alternative to more traditional, teacher-dominated reading activities.

The main focus of these chapters is on student independence. The real power of these questioning strategies will come when children are competent in using them, on their own, as necessary. Therefore, as you teach these critical strategies, it is important to show children how much they will increase their ability to really understand what they read. Children are *most* likely to internalize these strategies when they have had repeated opportunities to use them successfully in a variety of learning situations. Your students are then on their way to becoming highly proficient critical thinkers and readers.

All the strategies are presented in a consistent form: a rationale, a general description, and an example of the strategy used within the context of an actual lesson. In many instances, related information or an activity sheet is provided.

· · · ·

The ability to construct meaning from text and to gain content knowledge are both enhanced by thinking about and engaging in cross-curricular learning. In most content areas (Dupuis 1984), the process of constructing meaning has many of the same characteristics. Children construct meaning when

- what they are studying is authentic and important to them

- what they are learning integrates all the language arts—reading, writing, listening, speaking—as well as thinking

- their prior knowledge is tapped

- interrelationships between new knowledge and old knowledge, one curricular area and the other, are pointed out to them

- they have the support in *any* curricular area. Effective questions provide a way for teachers to offer this valuable assistance.

In chapter 7, I explore how questioning strategies can be used across the entire elementary curriculum, exhorting children to think critically and creatively in all content areas.

• • • •

## SOME GUIDELINES FOR USING QUESTIONING STRATEGIES

- *Use strategies on the basis of your students' needs.* Though the strategies are all motivational and teacher-tested, do not use them indiscriminately. Some students will have already picked up many effective reading and thinking strategies through their own experiences; they will not need the benefit of specific coaching in asking and answering questions. Use the questioning strategies only when you observe that meaning construction would be enhanced by a lesson on specific questioning techniques.

- *Introduce each questioning strategy in the context of an authentic educational experience.* Historically, there has been an unfortunate tendency for teachers to use strategies as isolated skills, dooming them to a reception of apathy and, eventually, failure. An authentic educational experience occurs when you (1) select motivational reading material from the integrated curriculum with which to use the strategy, (2) use this material as the vehicle through which to model the strategy, and (3) find other appropriate reading material with which the students may practice the strategy.

✦ *Introduce only one questioning strategy at a time.* To teach questioning strategies thoroughly, it is important that they be continually reinforced through practice with a variety of authentic reading experiences. The application of any new strategy is often difficult for children until it has been comfortably internalized; a lot of practice with one strategy at a time is the key to success.

✦ *Ensure that each student is successful using the strategy.* "Nothing succeeds like success." Children will feel successful using the questioning strategies if they have many opportunities to share how the strategies worked for them and if you point out their successes.

✦ *Strive to transfer the responsibility of the questioning strategies from you to the students.* In most of the questioning strategies, you must first model how the strategy is applied to reading material. Once the students feel comfortable using a strategy, you should fade from the picture and let children begin modeling it for each other, eventually using it independently. If, however, it becomes clear that more modeling is needed, reintroduce the strategy and provide guided practice, but return the responsibility to the students as quickly as possible (Cooper 1993).

# CHAPTER 3

# TEACHER QUESTIONING STRATEGIES FOR PRIMARY GRADES

**M**any educators still seem to believe both critical thinking and asking and answering higher-order questions are skills reserved for "older children"—those who have reached at least the fourth grade. Nothing could be further from the truth! The reality is that the sooner children begin to realize that there are many ways of thinking about an issue, the more likely it is that they will grow up with the freedom to look at the world in a variety of ways.

The strategies offered in this chapter can be begun with children as early as kindergarten, if no actual written response is required. Strategies that ask for written responses can be used as soon as students have the written proficiency to answer the questions, or they may be offered orally. Though suggested for the primary grades, these strategies are also appropriate for older students, particularly those who have had little previous practice in thinking critically.

## THE KNOWLEDGE CHART

### Rationale

Teachers can use this activity to show students how to access their background knowledge, or schema, through guided questions, then help them identify their new knowledge in a given subject by placing it on a chart. Modeled after a procedure developed by Ogle (1986), Knowledge Chart is intended to be used before and after reading or listening to a selection containing factual information. Informal evaluation reveals students are more likely to remember and recall information from a text when they used this activity because it has activated their schema, or framework of expectations, for the subject and provided a slot in which to assimilate new ideas. Moreover, the students' involvement and enthusiasm appear to increase when this technique is used (Yopp & Yopp 1992).

## Description

Draw five columns on the chalkboard or chart paper and head them: *Knowledge, Questions, New Knowledge, Research,* and *Reactions.* (Children in intermediate grades can fill in their own activity sheets. See figure 6, page 47.) Pick a topic, then have the students generate a list of all they know about that topic. Invite the students to ask questions about the topic; these questions serve as the guiding purposes for reading or listening. Next, read information about the chosen topic to the students, then record in a third column what they have learned about the subject as a result of having read or listened to the book or passage. (Students who are interested can use questions that have not been answered as questions for further research.) A fifth column is sometimes used to record reactions to learning that are particularly interesting, unusual, or unexpected. The procedure, in outline form, goes like this:

1. *Knowledge.* Ask the students: "What do you *know* about [*the topic*]?" Record all responses in the first column.

2. *Questions.* Ask: "What would you *like* to know about [*the topic*]?" Record the students' responses in the second column.

3. *New Knowledge.* After the reading, ask: "What have we learned about [*the topic*]?" Have the children revise *knowledge* listed in the first column, answer questions from the second column, and list new information that had not been considered prior to the reading.

4. *Research.* You can distribute student-initiated questions from the second column that have not been answered to interested students for further investigation.

5. *Reactions.* Ask a question that will lead students to a personal evaluation, such as: "How did this story change your feelings or thinking about [*the topic*]?"

### Example

Second-grade children, about to read about kookaburras, were asked: "What do you know about kookaburras?" Their teacher wrote their responses in the first column of the knowledge chart:

+ It's an animal.
+ They are found in zoos.
+ They live in gum trees.
+ There is a song about them.

Next the teacher asked: "Is there anything you would like to know about kookaburras?" She wrote the children's responses in the second column of the knowledge chart:

+ What do they eat?
+ Where do they live?
+ Do they make good pets?
+ Are they friendly?
+ What kind of animal are they?
+ Do they have fur?
+ Who are their enemies?
+ Can you keep them as pets?

Then the teacher reviewed the questions that the children had asked and had them read the following paragraph to see if they could find the answers to their questions.

### The Kookaburra

The kookaburra lives in Australia. It lives in the forest in small groups. Kookaburras are very friendly. They will accept food from people. Sometimes they even tap on windows hoping that people will feed them. Kookaburras eat insects, crabs, fish, and small birds. They are also quite famous as snake killers.

After the reading, the teacher asked the children to revisit the knowl-edge chart to see if any of their original understandings about kookaburras had been changed (no). She then asked them to see if any of their questions about kookaburras had been answered (three had and they could make inferences about others from the information in the passage).

At this point, the teacher asked the children to share some entirely new information they had learned about kookaburras from reading the passage. She listed the children's responses in the third column of the knowledge chart:

+ They are famous snake killers.
+ They beg for food.
+ They live in small groups.

Of the original questions that the children had asked, at least two were not answered at all. A group of interested children were sent to the library to search for the answers to the following questions noted in the knowledge chart:

+ What kind of animals are the kookaburra?
+ Do they have fur?
+ Who are their enemies?
+ Can you keep them as pets?

Finally, the teacher asked for the students' reactions to the passage: "How did this paragraph change your thinking or feelings about the kookaburra?" She wrote the following students' responses on the knowl-edge chart:

+ I heard the kookaburra song before and I had always wondered what that was.
+ Now I know it's a funny animal.
+ I want to read *more* about kookaburras!
+ I think from reading that Australia must be a cool place.
+ I want to go there sometime.

## The Knowledge Chart

Name **Sarah, Charles, José**          Date **Sept. 18**

Topic **Seahorses**

| Knowledge | Questions | New Knowledge | Research | Reactions |
|---|---|---|---|---|
| What do you know about Seahorses? | What do you want to know about Seahorses? | What did you discover after reading about Seahorses? | What do you still want to know about Seahorses? | How do you now think or feel about Seahorses? |
| The seahorse is not really a horse. | Where can you find them? | Male seahorses give birth, and care for the babies. | Do they have live babies? | I am more curious about them. |
| They live in salty seas. | What do they eat? | Both eyes can see independently. | How can we keep them from becoming extinct? | I feel sad that they are losing their habitat. |
| They're fish. | Are they endangered? | They live in coral reefs, sea grass beds, and mangroves. | How can we clean up their habitat? | We are going to write a letter to the president to ask him to stop polluting coastal waters where the seahorse lives. |
| They have curly tails. | Could you keep them as pets? | There are 35 different kinds, or species. | If the males give birth, are they really males? | |
| They hang on to weeds. | What are their predators? | They are endangered. | How long do they live? | |
| They are very tiny. | Do they come in different colors? | They are used for food, medicine, and decoration in many countries. | | |
| They don't swim in schools | | Pollution is destroying the seahorse's habitat. | | |
| | | Their predators are larger fishes, crabs, and waterbirds. | | |

*Figure 6. Knowledge Chart Activity Sheet*
Knowledge Chart filled in by grade 5 students

✦ I want to go to the zoo and see if they have a real kookaburra.

✦ I used to think kookaburra was just a weird word; now I can imagine what one looks like.

### Related Information

It is important that you restrict the use of the Knowledge Chart to books that contain factual information, or those with expository text. For example, children gain little, if any, accurate information about bears from reading *Goldilocks and the Three Bears,* which is narrative text. However, some works of fiction, or narrative text, do contain factual information in a most palatable format. In *The Secret Garden,* for instance, children learn much about the English moors. Thus, you must be familiar with the reading material and certain that it provides accurate factual information about the topic before using it as a subject for a knowledge chart.

## RESPONSE HEURISTIC

### Rationale

Often teachers have children write in reading response or dialogue journals and are frustrated at the students' lack of personal involvement in the story or passage. Students often parrot, not react to, the events in the story; for example, "Leslie hit her head on a rock while crossing the river" instead of "Leslie died and I felt I had lost a friend. It reminded me of how sad and lonely I felt when my grandmother died." By modeling the appropriate critical questions that students should be asking, teachers can encourage their students to respond to the text on a deeper and more personal level. The Response Heuristic, developed by Bleich (1978), provides a means for students to analyze their own thoughts and feelings and helps them get into the habit of asking pertinent questions as they read.

## Description

This questioning strategy involves three components: perceptions, reactions, and associations. It is helpful to introduce the strategy by modeling it with a story that has just been read to or by students. They then give their own personal responses to each questioning component: (1) perceptions ("What is important in the book?"); (2) reactions ("How does the story make you feel?"); and (3) associations ("What experiences have you had that the story reminds you of?").

After an initial teacher-modeled, shared reading experience using this technique, children can begin to write their own responses using an activity sheet (see figure 7, page 50.) Encourage the students to share their responses and affirm it is possible to have many different "correct" responses to the same material.

## Example

A third-grade class listened to *A Christmas Sonata,* by Gary Paulsen, a story about a young boy whose faith has been restored in the spirit of the season. The following are one student's reactions to the story:

1. *Perceptions*

   TEACHER: What is important in the book?

   STUDENT: Everything was going wrong for the boy and it looked like he was going to have a rotten Christmas. Santa Claus is the spirit of Christmas. Santa Claus was real for the boy. The boy's mother was real poor and his friend was dying of leukemia.

2. *Reactions*

   TEACHER: How did the story make you feel?

   STUDENT: I was happy *and* sad at the end because his friend Matthew died, but he was happy about Santa Claus. Sad for Matthew because he suffered a lot. Surprised when there really was a Santa Claus at the end; at least, that's what you were supposed to think. I

**Response Heuristic**

**Name** Claudia **Date** December 10

**Book Title** Ramona Quimby, Age 8 by Beverly Cleary

1. What is important in the book?

Ramona has to do lots of things she has never done before. She's trying to be brave but it's hard for her.

2. How does the story make you feel?

I feel sorry for Ramona when she was getting so upset. She had to put up with her four year old sister too. I felt proud of Ramona that she could do it and when the old man said she had a nice family, I was happy for Ramona.

3. What experiences have you had that the story reminds you of?

When my mother had to go back to work we all had to stick together. I didn't like it when she was never home when I got there. I can understand how Ramona felt.

Reproducible master in appendix

*Figure 7. Response Heuristic Activity Sheet*

Students in intermediate grades fill in their own activity sheets was excited when Santa Claus really came because I remembered how I used to feel at Christmas time when I was little and still believed in him.

3. *Associations*

TEACHER: What experiences have you had that the story reminds you of?

STUDENT: When I was six, I think, my grandpa died the week before Christmas. I was really sad because he was like my best friend. What was even worse was that everybody else was in a sad mood and Christmas just wasn't the way it's supposed to be—happy. We got presents and stuff but it wasn't the same. It was different in the book, though, because the boy had a great Christmas anyway. I don't remember anything good about the Christmas when my grandpa died.

## POLAR OPPOSITES

### Rationale

This questioning activity is ideal for helping children see characters in texts as three-dimensional. This is done by asking them to assess characters on a variety of traits, using a three-, five-, or seven-point scale, depending on the grade level of the students. (It is difficult enough for young children to pick one of three choices; older children can judge more nuances of meaning on a five- or seven-choice scale.) The exercise is most conducive to critical thinking when students are also asked to justify their responses. In other words, if they rate a character *generous* rather than *frugal,* the teacher asks them why they believe this to be so, reminding them to cite evidence from the selection read to support their position.

**Polar Opposites Chart**

Name  Ho A, JARED, Michael, Emily      Date  March 22

Book Title  Miss Maggie

Where do you think  Nat  would fit on this chart for each of these traits?

1. brave  __  X  __  __  __  fearful

I think Nat was fearful at first but he overcame his fear when he went in Miss Maggie's house.

2. cautious  X  __  __  __  adventurous

Nat was very cautious. Even though he went in Miss Maggie's house, it said his heart was pounding in his chest. I don't think he likes exploring.

3. wise  __  __  X  __  __  foolish

Nat was foolish to believe all these things about Miss Maggie that were all lies, But he was wise enough to change his mind and care about her later.

4. happy  __  X  __  __  __  sad

You don't ever see Nat laughing or having fun but he doesn't seem unhappy anywhere.

5. generous  X  __  __  __  __  greedy

Nat is very generous to share his family and their love with Miss Maggie.

6. a leader  __  __  __  X  __  a follower

Nat shouldn't listen to what people say so much or he could have had Miss Maggie as a wonderful friend much sooner.

*Figure 8. Polar Opposites Activity Sheet*

## Description

To initiate Polar Opposites, choose a character from a story all the students are familiar with and develop a list of personality traits that describes that character. Then determine an opposite quality for each of the traits. For example, if a character is quiet and thoughtful and tends to stay by himself, you might write on one side of the chart *loner, quiet,* and *considerate.* On the opposite side of the chart, then, you may include the words *fun-loving, noisy,* and *inconsiderate.* Each pair of opposites comprises its own continuum, with three, five, or seven spaces in between (see figure 8). The students (as a group or individually) must determine where on the continuum each character falls. You then read the story or passage, and ask the children the following for each character: "Where do you think [*character*] would fit on this character chart? Why do you think so? What in the story supports your answer?"

## Example

A grade-three teacher read *Miss Maggie,* by Cynthia Rylant, to her students. The book is about Nat, a young boy who has heard stories about the reclusive elderly lady who lives in the log hut on his family's property; a big black snake, among other scary things, is reputed to live with her. Nat, initially fearing Miss Maggie, looks in her window and then runs away. One day he overcomes his fears when he finds her in trouble: in the heart of winter, she is without heat. He finds her sitting on the floor of her cabin clutching a dead starling. He runs to get help for her. His family begins taking care of her and taking her with them on outings. Nat establishes a special, caring relationship with Miss Maggie.

After the reading, the activity sheet on page 52 (figure 8) was completed by some of the students.

## MULTIPLE RESPONSE STRATEGY

### Rationale

The use of the Multiple Response Strategy (Orlich et al. 1985) is a logical precursor to student-conducted discussions. Student discussions, however, are difficult to use effectively because young children do not always possess the needed discussion behaviors or skills. By using multiple response questions, the teacher subtly conditions the students to accept more and more responsibility for listening to one another and for modifying modeled responses. Additionally, by using divergent or critical questions coupled with the Multiple Response Strategy, the teacher has a unique opportunity to analyze the types of responses that are being given and can make a qualitative evaluation of each learner's response.

### Description

Using the Multiple Response Strategy, at least three or four students may answer a given question. The key to increasing the number of students who respond to a question is to ask a divergent (creative) or evaluative (critical) question, or one that is open-ended. By doing this, you can predict there will be more than one response or that responses will not duplicate one another. Moreover, you will not have a preconceived notion of what the *correct* answer should be. Proceed with the strategy as follows:

1. Create either a divergent or evaluative question.

2. Pose the question to the class.

3. Provide adequate time for all learners to consider the question, articulate a response, and raise their hands.

4. Identify three or four students to offer responses.

5. Caution students that they must listen carefully to their classmates' responses, so they will not repeat what has been previously offered.

6. After the children have responded, praise them for different reasons (for example, one student for providing the most complete

response, another for the most original response, and yet another for the best response obtained from an encyclopedia).

## Example

A second-grade teacher used the Multiple Response Strategy to encourage children to listen to one another as they considered a critical-thinking question.

TEACHER: Today I'm going to try something new. I'll ask a question, wait for a minute for everyone to think about it, and then I'll call on four of you to respond. You will need to listen very carefully because I will not repeat the question. Also, you will need to listen very carefully to your classmates as they answer so that you don't repeat what they have said. (*Asks a student to paraphrase the instructions to be sure everyone understood.*) Here goes. (*Asks question in anticipation for a unit on eyesight.*) Why do you think we have two eyes instead of only one? (*Pauses*) José, Gina, Chrissy, Hoa.

JOSÉ: Well, we have two arms and two legs and even two eyebrows. I think we would look silly with just one eye! (*Teacher nods head, smiles, and points to Gina without commenting.*)

GINA: Yeah, but we only have one nose and one mouth. We're *used* to it being that way. What if we had two mouths? (*The other children laugh. The teacher nods and points to Chrissy.*)

CHRISSY: Because God made us this way. That's the only reason why.

HOA: Well, maybe God made us with two eyes in case one didn't work. My uncle is blind in one eye. If he didn't have another eye he would not be able to see at all.

TEACHER: Those are all interesting ideas. Children, let's see what we can find out about our eyesight in the library. I will check the encyclopedia. Graciela and Jacques, you see if you can find a trade book about our eyes and eyesight.

## RECIPROCAL TEACHING

### Rationale

Reciprocal Teaching, developed by Palinscar and Brown (1984), encourages students to monitor their own comprehension while reading expository text. It also encourages students to be active in the process of constructing meaning from texts. Proficient readers often stop during the reading of expository text to see what questions have been answered and what new questions have arisen as a result of the reading, even though such questions are asked instantaneously and subconsciously. Students can be shown through Reciprocal Teaching that while reading answers questions, it also often generates *new* questions.

### Description

During Reciprocal Teaching, model the comprehension activity, and then have the students attempt the same activity, with feedback from you on their performance. Specifically, the outline of the procedure is as follows:

1. With the students, read a passage of expository text aloud.

2. Ask the group an important question about the text, one that focuses upon the key issue.

3. Model this question-asking process for the students many times.

4. When the group is ready to ask the questions, guide their questions and give feedback on the questions.

5. Model, praise correct responses, ask probing questions, and, generally, offer feedback.

6. Together, with the students, select from four main critical-thinking strategies: (1) summarize the section that was read, (2) predict what the next section will be about, (3) ask a question about the main idea of the section that was read, and (4) ask a question that helps to clarify the meaning of the passage.

**Example**

The following dialogue between a teacher and a small group of third-grade students who had read a passage about koala bears indicates the type of progress that can be made using Reciprocal Teaching.

JARED: What is found in Australia and also eucalyptus leaves and they have…No, this isn't right.

TEACHER: Do you want to ask a question about koala bears?

JARED: Yeah.

TEACHER: Well, what would be a good question to ask about them that starts with the word *why?*

JARED: Why do they want to be koala bears…no…

TEACHER: You're on the right track. Try again.

JARED: Why are they called *koala bears?*

TEACHER: There you go. Good for you. They are called koala bears because they look like little bears. Would they make good pets?

MARTA: No, even though they are cute, they are wild animals and they live in trees. My turn? Are they extinct…are they in danger of becoming extinct?

TEACHER: Great question! No, it says that koala bears are protected animals. I think that means that they are in no immediate danger. I predict it will tell us in the next paragraph that they are in no danger of becoming extinct. I also predict it will tell us who their enemies are.

## PROBABLE PASSAGES

### Rationale

Karen Wood's article "Probable Passages: A Writing Strategy" (1987) is a teacher-modeled prediction strategy that integrates writing and critical thinking with the reading of narrative selections. Such a strategy enables students to use their understanding of the six story elements—setting, beginning, problem, attempt, outcome, and original story ending—to construct text using key words provided by the teacher. This strategy features a unique marriage of knowledge of story grammar and prereading prediction to encourage critical thinking.

### Description

This strategy is divided into four stages: (1) the preparation stage, (2) the prereading stage, (3) the reading stage, and (4) the post-reading stage. The strategy is conducted in the following manner.

1. *Preparation Stage.* On the chalkboard or overhead, write *Key Words, Story Frame,* and *Blank Probable Passage.* Select a passage of narrative (story) text and pick out words that are important to the problem. List these words under *Key Words.* Next, write the six story elements under *Story Frame.* In *Blank Probable Passage,* set up a fill-in-the-blanks passage. This passage must include the story grammar:

   The story takes place [*setting*]. [*Beginning*] is a character in the story who _____ . A problem occurs when [*problem*]. Then [*attempt*]. The problem is solved when [*outcome*]. The story ends [*ending*].

2. *Prereading Stage.* Read the key words aloud and ask the students to repeat them. Ask these questions: "What do you think a story that uses these words is going to be about? How would these words fit into the story frame?" Then help the students use the words from the story frame to complete a logical probable passage.

3. *Reading Stage.* Have the students read the selection to find out how close their predictions match the actual story.

4. *Post-Reading Stage.* Ask: "How did your probable passage compare with the plot of the story?" Have students revise the probable passage to reflect the actual story plot. (Note: Often the students' probable passage turns out to be a more interesting story than the *actual* one. Point this out.)

**Example**

A second-grade class used the Probable Passages strategy with Hans Wilhelm's *Bunny Trouble.*

1. *Preparation Stage*
   The teacher wrote the key words, the story frame, and a blank probable passage on the chalkboard (see figure 9a, page 60).

2. *Prereading Stage*
   The teacher read the key words aloud, asking the children to repeat them after her. She explained the meanings of terms and words, such as *rabbit colony, nuisance,* and *overtime,* that the children were unfamiliar with. She then said to the children: "Think about these words and see if you can come up with a story in your mind using as many of the words as you can."

   Next, she drew children's attention to the story frame and reviewed the major elements in narrative or story structure. She asked them to place the key words into the appropriate places in the story frame. Then, she had them write the words, as they had already been organized in the story frame, to complete a logical Probable Passage (see figure 9b, page 60).

3. *Reading Stage*
   The teacher directed the students: "Read this story to see how the story compares with how you thought the story might be."

*Figure 9a.*
*Probable Passages:*
*Preparation Stage*
*for* **Bunny Trouble**

Probable Passages: Preparation Stage

Key Words

| | | |
|---|---|---|
| rabbit colony | soccer-crazy | trouble |
| Easter | nuisance | plan |
| decorating | worried | promise |
| deliver | overtime | cage |
| design | Ralph | free |

Story Frame

Probable Passages: Prereading Stage

| Setting | Beginning | Problem | Attempt | Outcome | Ending |
|---|---|---|---|---|---|
| rabbit colony | Easter decorating design | Soccer-crazy trouble nuisance | deliver plan | worried cage | free promise |

Probable Passage for ___Bunny Trouble___

The story takes place _in a rabbit colony_. _Ralph_ is a character in the story who _is soccer-crazy_. A problem occurs when _it is Easter time and the rabbits have to decorate eggs_. Then _Ralph gets into trouble. He gets kidnapped while he is playing soccer and somebody gets him and puts him in a cage_. The problem is solved when _Ralph gets his friends to help him break out of the cage_. The story ends _with Ralph promising never to play soccer again_.

*Figure 9b. Probable Passages: Prereading Stage*

4. *Post-Reading Stage*

The teacher asked: "How did the actual story compare with your prediction?" The children agreed their probable passage was very close to the actual story. Finally, the teacher asked the children to complete a blank Probable Passage using the actual story (see figure 9c, page 62).

## Related Information

Wood recommends that after guiding the children through several Probable Passages, you should encourage them to work in small cooperative groups to create their own Probable Passages. The small groups can then share their predictive stories with the rest of the class and decide for themselves, after reading the story, which of the groups' passages was closest to the actual story. Similarly, the revised Probable Passages can be composed in the same small groups and shared with the class as a whole.

## Probable Passages: Postreading Stage

**Name** _Nicole_ **Date** _Jan. 20_

**Book Title** _Bunny Trouble_

### Revised Probable Passage

The story takes place _in a rabbit colony in a forest._

_____ _Ralph_ _____ is a character in the story who _only cares about soccer and doesn't help the other bunnies decorate the eggs for Easter._

A problem occurs when _Ralph goes off to play soccer by himself on the other side of the forest. A farmer catches him, puts him in a cage and is going to make him be Easter dinner._

Then _everyone in the rabbit colony is worried about him and his mother cries._

The problem is solved when _his sister Liza squeezes a basket of beautiful eggs into his cage. The farmer's children guess he must be the Easter bunny and beg their father to let him go._

The story ends _with Ralph running home. He still plays soccer but now he also helps the other bunnies._

*Figure 9c. Probable Passages: Postreading Stage*
Older children can fill in their own revised Probable Passage

# CHAPTER 4

# TEACHER QUESTIONING STRATEGIES FOR INTERMEDIATE GRADES

C hildren in the intermediate grades are busy exploring new ideas about themselves and the world around them. They often amaze their teachers with their zealous intellectual curiosity—when the "right" questions are asked of them. When we depart from simple factual recall and begin asking children what they think, feel, and believe, the classroom atmosphere becomes palpably "charged" and is an exciting place to be.

The questioning activities in this chapter are appropriate for children who have some clearly developed writing skill, those who have had practice with the type of critical and creative thinking required by the activities in chapter 3, or for primary-age children who are eager for a more potent intellectual challenge.

## THINK ALOUD

### Rationale

The Think Aloud is one of the most effective ways for a teacher to model critical questioning. This strategy shows, specifically, how a proficient reader uses a variety of reading skills to construct meaning from text. In addition to knowing about particular reading strategies, readers need to know when and why they work. Teachers model all these skills in the Think Aloud as they show students what *they* do as *they* read. When students learn to control and guide their reading, they are much more likely to become proficient readers (Baker & Brown 1984).

### Description

In the Think Aloud strategy, developed by Davey (1983), you read a passage aloud, and, at the same time, give the students an opportunity to *hear* your thoughts by verbalizing the strategies—making comments and asking probing questions—a fluent reader uses to derive meaning. Davey offers five techniques proficient readers use for thinking critically and processing the text:

1. hypothesizing and predicting
2. organizing images
3. using prior knowledge
4. monitoring one's own understanding
5. rectifying comprehension errors

You can model the Think Aloud strategy in the following way:

1. Beforehand, either make copies of the text passage you will demonstrate with, or prepare to show it on an overhead projector. Explain to the students that they can follow what you *read* but that you will also "think aloud" so that they can *hear* your thoughts.

2. Read the passage aloud while the students follow along. (The passage should be somewhat difficult for the children, with concepts and vocabulary slightly above the reading level of the learners.)

3. As you read aloud, talk through the strategies you are using to figure out vocabulary through the context, to decipher obscure phrases, or to relate the ideas in the text with those you are familiar with.

4. After modeling several paragraphs, invite the students to add their own problem-solving tactics and personal impressions to your thought processes.

After you have modeled several Think Alouds, provide the children with short passages of similar difficulty and encourage them to try Think Aloud with partners, rotating the oral reading and taking turns adding to the other person's thinking process. As students become adept at thinking aloud with partners, give them opportunities to read selected passages individually and to practice the newly learned thinking skills silently.

So that the children focus on the appropriate thinking procedures when they are using the strategy silently, have them ask themselves the following questions:

1. After looking at the cover, the title, and the pictures (if any) in this passage, what do I think it is going to be about? (*hypothesizing and predicting*)

2. What is going on right now in the passage? (to be asked at least after every paragraph) (*organizing images*)

3. What am I reminded of here that I already know about? (*using prior knowledge*)

4. What do I think these unfamiliar words might mean? What are some ways I can get clues to their meaning? (*monitoring one's own understanding*)

5. Do I want to change any of my original thinking as I read? (to be asked after every paragraph) (*rectifying comprehension errors*)

### Example

The teacher read aloud a paragraph about lemmings from a passage entitled "The Mystery of the Lemmings." It tells about the lemmings' strange rush to the sea, which results in their drowning, and then questions why the animals would exhibit this behavior. These are the strategies modeled by the teacher as she read the passage aloud:

1. *Hypothesizing.* "'The Mystery of the Lemmings.' Hmmm. I really like mysteries and they usually have some unsolved puzzle in them. I know that lemmings are small animals; I wonder what could be

mysterious about them? Maybe they have some strange habits, like ostriches that bury their heads in the sand, or chameleons that change color."

2. *Organizing images.* "As I read along, I see that these little animals rush to the sea to drown themselves! At first I thought they must be running away to seek better feeding grounds, but it's not that because it says they pass by many of the things that they like to eat. I'm getting the idea that they don't know why they are going."

3. *Using prior knowledge.* "The description of the animals being about five inches long and with light brown fur reminds me of hamsters, or maybe gerbils. Probably lemmings are in the rodent family, although it doesn't say that."

4. *Monitoring understanding.* "As I read along I'm changing what I first thought about why these animals drown themselves. I have confirmed what I thought—it's *not* for food—but I think maybe they *do* know why. I realized when it says that some stay back to start a family that not all of them go. Maybe it's like bees, in that certain lemmings have certain tasks and they just seem to know what those tasks are."

5. *Rectifying errors.* "The first picture in my mind when it mentioned lemmings drowning themselves in the sea was some kind of starving, unhappy colony of animals that didn't want to live anymore. Then I began to think maybe they are like sheep and just followed the first one blindly. I'm changing my mind about that because of new information about feeding grounds and some lemmings staying behind. I think now that maybe these animals march to the sea for much the same reason that birds fly south for the winter—I have read that some inner clock or *instinct* is why birds fly south. Perhaps the same instinct is what makes the lemmings rush to the sea."

## Activity Sheet

After you have modeled many Think Alouds in various curricular areas, encourage students to crystallize their own Think Aloud questions and monitoring strategies, using an activity sheet (see figure 10). (The activity sheet should be phased out as the students internalize the strategy.)

---

**Think Aloud**

Name _____   Date _____

Story Title _____

1. How often did I ask myself what I thought this story or paragraph was about?

        never     sometimes     often     after every paragraph

2. How often did I see pictures in my mind of what was going on?

        never     sometimes     often     after every paragraph

3. How often did what I read remind me of something else that I know about?

        never     sometimes     often     after every paragraph

4. How often did I stop to see if I was understanding what was going on in the story or paragraph?

        never     sometimes     often     after every paragraph

5. How often did I change what I had originally thought about what was going on in the story or passage?

        never     sometimes     often     after every paragraph

---

*Reproducible master in appendix*

*Figure 10. Think Aloud Activity Sheet*

## QUESTION-ELICITING QUESTIONS

### Rationale

Singer's (1978) strategy for promoting self-questioning emanates from a modeling strategy that teachers may use to encourage children to ask questions, thus setting their own purposes for reading. Singer postulates that when students, not teachers, set the purposes for reading, they become more engaged in the search for answers. When consistently used, children internalize the self-questioning strategies and begin to construct text the way proficient readers do.

### Description

Singer outlines three components for guiding comprehension through questions: (1) modeling, (2) phase-in/phase-out, and (3) critical thinking:

1. *Modeling.* Ask questions to determine what the children want to know.

2. *Phase-in/phase-out.* After modeling appropriate questions, write the questions students have about the text on the chalkboard or overhead. At this stage, you are phasing out your role as questioner and phasing the students in.

3. *Critical thinking.* Through your guidance, students learn to ask critical-thinking questions about the text in order to construct their own meanings.

### Example

The teacher took the story, *Earl's Too Cool for Me,* by Leah Komaiko, and read the title aloud.

Then she asked her first question-eliciting question: "What do you want to know after hearing just the title of this book?" Children responded with several questions, which the teacher duly recorded on the chalkboard:

+ What does Earl do that is cool?
+ Who is Earl?
+ Who is telling the story about Earl?
+ Is Earl an animal or a human?
+ How old is Earl?

The teacher then read the first three lines of the story aloud:

> Earl's got a bicycle made of hay.
> He takes rides on the Milky Way.
> Earl's Too Cool for me.

She asked a second question: "What would you like to know about Earl now?" The students responded with the following:

+ Is Earl real?
+ Is the person telling the story making it up?
+ Does Earl ever get hurt?
+ What else does Earl do?
+ Is Earl a nice person?

The teacher then asked: "Is there anything you would like to ask the author of this story?" (The questions you ask, of course, depend on the content of the story.) The students responded with:

+ What happens next?
+ What else does Earl do that is cool?
+ Where did the author get the idea for this story?
+ Why did she choose this title?
+ Does she think Earl is cool?
+ Does the author like "cool" people?

## EXPERIENCE-TEXT-RELATIONSHIP (ETR)

### Rationale

Students cannot always relate their experiences to a topic before reading. Their background must be brought to bear at all phases of the reading process through effective teacher questioning. Kathryn Au has had great success helping diverse learners achieve in reading by making the past experiences of each child an integral part of the entire lesson. In Au's ETR method (Au 1979; Cecil 1993), children practice expressing complex thoughts; as they respond to questions, the teacher gets an idea of which steps are easy or difficult for individual children. Through the teacher's questioning, cuing, and prompting, the students are able to integrate features of the new story with their existing understandings of the world. Children who have interacted frequently with a teacher in ETR are better able to think critically than those who have not been afforded this opportunity.

### Description

Au's critical-thinking lessons are composed of three different kinds of sequences: (1) an *experience* sequence for eliciting background; (2) a *text* sequence for determining what meaning the children are deriving from the material; and (3) a *relationship* sequence, in which children compare their own experiences with what they have just read. The lesson proceeds as follows:

1. *Experience.* Ask children questions about experiences they have had, or ask them to share certain knowledge they have that is directly related to the story they will soon read or hear.

2. *Text.* After all children have had an opportunity to share their knowledge or experience, have them read or listen to short passages from the story (usually a page or two at a time), asking them critical-thinking questions about the content after each section is read. Sometimes the responses reveal the children's misunderstandings, due to their differing world views, and you must then add the necessary background information to correct the misunderstanding.

3. *Relationship.* At this point, attempt to make connections for the children between the content of the story, as discussed in the text sequence (#2), and their own outside experiences and knowledge, as shared in the experience sequence (#1).

### Example

A fourth-grade teacher guided her students through an ETR sequence, incorporating Jay William's story, *The Practical Princess*, about an unorthodox princess with a good deal of common sense. The teacher, concerned that the author's clever use of satire may be misinterpreted by the children, felt ETR (because of its constant questioning) was the best strategy to help the children better appreciate the story.

1. *Experience.* Before reading the story, the teacher asked the students to share experiences and knowledge that they thought might relate to the story they were about to read.

   TEACHER: Do any of you know what it means to be *practical?* Can you give me an example of someone, or something you or someone else has done, that could be considered practical?

   NICOLE: Well, once my sister asked my mother if she would like a mink coat for her birthday. I remember she answered that she already had a coat, and a microwave would be more practical.

   RAÚL: I went camping one time and my uncle said to wear practical shoes. He meant, I think, not my Sunday-best ones, just sturdy ones.

   TEACHER: Those are both very good examples. Nicole, your mother wanted a microwave because she would use it more—it would be more sensible for her than a mink coat. Raúl, you were advised to wear practical shoes—not fancy ones that wouldn't be sensible. Now I'd like us to read a story about a princess who is not like some of the princesses you may have read about. She is not always concerned with fine jewelry and clothes; instead, she is constantly using her head to get out of bad situations. Let's find out what she does that makes her seem so practical.

2. *Text.* As the children read several paragraphs at a time, the teacher stopped them periodically to discuss the text. By probing their thinking as they were reading, the teacher tried to clear up any misunderstandings, and modeled how a proficient reader can think through confusing parts.

TEACHER: Why do you think the princess says to the dragon that he only wants to marry her because he's a snob?

RANA: Who would want to marry a dragon? She's probably waiting for Prince Charming (*other children laugh*).

TEACHER: Well, that's what happens in lots of fairy tales, isn't it, Rana? But it might be that this princess has another reason for not wanting to get married. Does the dragon really love the princess, do you think?

NICOLE: Uh uh. He just thinks he has to marry a princess because princesses are supposed to be so cool! That's why she thinks the dragon is a snob. He just cares too much what other people think.

TEACHER: Good thinking, Nicole. He doesn't care at all what she is like as long as she's a princess. How do you feel about this kind of thinking?

3. *Relationship.* Having cleared up several confusions similar to the one cited in the previous sequence, the teacher was now confident that the children had gained a fuller appreciation of the tale. She was ready to relate the story with the students' prior experiences and knowledge.

TEACHER: Have you ever known anyone who used her head to get out of bad experiences the way Princess Bedelia did?

RANA: Yeah, the woman in *Alien II.* She led everyone to safety using her smarts (*others laugh*). Princesses are usually too busy being beautiful to use their brains. Look at Princess Di! It was cool the way Princess Bedelia did, though. She could have just gone along with it and married the dragon the way everyone expected her to.

TEACHER: Yes—that is what we have come to expect in fairy tales, isn't it? How did you like how she managed to keep from marrying the dragon?

NICOLE: That was really cool. She got him to come out of the cave by telling him to come and get her, and then she blew him up. Kerpow! That's sort of like how I trick my dog to get him to take a bath. He hides under the bed when he sees the hose, so I bribe him with a dog biscuit (*the others laugh*).

RANA: It sounds like *you* use your common sense to get your dog in the bathtub!

TEACHER: Yes! I guess Nicole is *practical* sometimes too, right?

## SCAMPERing

### Rationale

Eberle (1984) originally devised a technique by which teachers can help children understand how to generate new ideas by linking them with existing ones. It is useful as a prewriting questioning strategy used in conjunction with any story from a basal reader or trade book. It is also an enrichment tool that can be used to increase the flexibility of students' thinking about stories and to improve their divergent thinking skills.

### Description

SCAMPER is an acronym that describes the quest for ideas and images about stories that have previously been read. Each letter in the word is the first letter of the name of a creative-thinking technique included in the process: **S**ubstitute, **C**ombine, **A**dapt, **M**odify/Magnify, **P**ut to use/ Point of view, **E**liminate, **R**earrange/Reverse. These techniques generate thought-provoking questions to create exciting, new stories.

+ Substitute: What item or event in the story can be changed to another item or event? How would this substitution change the whole story?

+ Combine: What characters from other stories would you like to add to this one to change the events in the story? How will the story turn out now?

+ Adapt: How could the results of one conversation or event lead to a different ending to this story?

+ Modify: What event can be changed so that the story has a different ending?

+ Magnify: What will happen to the characters after the story has ended?

+ Put to Use: How can you give a character more to do or say in the story, or how can some item be used more than it was?

+ Point of View: How would the story be different if it were told by one of the other characters?

+ Eliminate: What would happen if you got rid of one of the main characters in the story?

+ Rearrange: Change the order of events in this story. How will this affect the ending?

+ Reverse: Give the main characters the opposite personality traits. How will the story be different if the good characters become bad, and the bad characters become good?

### Example

A teacher used the SCAMPERing technique to help children think about the story, *The Three Billy Goats Gruff,* in fresh and original ways through thought-provoking questions that will culminate in a written response.

✦ *Substitute: Substitute one item in the story for another.* "What might have happened if the billy goats had had to go through a tunnel instead of crossing a bridge?"

✦ *Combine: Combine characters from the story or from another story and compare them and revise the story accordingly.* "What would happen if the three goats joined forces with the three little pigs?"

✦ *Adapt: Make an adaptation of a character's behavior or of a plot feature.* "What might have happened if the three billy goats had attempted to cross the bridge at the same time?"

✦ *Modify: Change or modify an element of the plot.* "What do you think the troll might have done if the goats had made no noise crossing the bridge?"

✦ *Magnify: Extend the story.* "What do you think will happen in the goats' lives, now that they are safely on the other side of the bridge?"

✦ *Put to Use: Intensify the role of some element or character in the story.* "In what other ways might the goats have used their horns?"

✦ *Point of View: Rewrite the story from the point of view of a different character.* "How would the story be different through the eyes of the troll?"

✦ *Eliminate: Get rid of one of the major characters.* "How would the story be different if there were no troll?"

✦ *Rearrange: Change the sequence of events.* "Imagine the largest billy goat had crossed the bridge first. How would the ending of the story change?"

✦ *Reverse: Switch the prominent personality characteristics of the main characters.* "How would you rewrite the story if the peace-loving troll is trying to cross the bridge but the three irritable goats won't let him?"

---

**SCAMPERing**

Name ___Greta___ Date ___Jan 8___

Book Title ___The Three Little Pigs___

To rewrite the story in a new way, select a question, then answer it in the
space at the bottom (turn the page if you need more room).

1. **Substitute:** What might have happened if the three little pigs had been
camping rather than living in houses?

2. **Combine:** What would happen ~~...~~ iding Hood and the wolf
joined the three lit~~...~~

3. **Adapt:** What might have ha~~...~~
the police?

4. **Modify:** What might have b~~...~~
couldn't blow?

5. **Magnify:** What do you thi~~...~~
the wolf is gov~~...~~

6. **Put to Use:** In what othe~~...~~
abilities to co~~...~~

7. **Point of View:** How would~~...~~
of the wo~~...~~

8. **Eliminate:** How would~~...~~
come along~~...~~

9. **Rearrange:** How would~~...~~
house but t~~...~~

10. **Reverse:** How would ~~...~~
trying to bl~~...~~

**Answer:** __Magnify__

The last we saw the~~...~~

were jumping up a~~...~~

down the chimney~~...~~

whose brick hous~~...~~

him, because Mr. Wolf had completely destroyed their
houses. So they moved in. They had a big party and
invited all their friends. Things were great for a while.
Then Oscar started to get really annoyed that he was
the only one cleaning up after himself. He was
James and Freddy three warnings, but they would
never help. So finally Oscar kicked them out. For
three weeks they were homeless. Then they got an
idea. They went to Oscar's house one night, pretending
to be a wolf, with both of them huffing and puffing,
they really sounded just like the wolf. Oscar freaked.
He started running around shouting, "James! Freddy!
Help! I'm in trouble!" "Freddy and James flung open
the door and yelled, "It's just us!." At first Oscar was
mad, but then he got over it. He was relieved to not
see the wolf that he told James and Freddy they could
stay. They promised they would help clean up. As
far as I know, all three pigs are still living
together.

*Figure 11. SCAMPERing Activity Sheet*
A student creates a new ending to *The Three Little Pigs*

# FICTIONAL ROLE-PLAYS

## Rationale

Proficient readers infuse intellectual and emotional meanings into text. The particular definitions and associations the words in a book have for each reader determine exactly what the message communicates to him and greatly enhance the meaning of text and the enjoyment of reading. Thus, it is important for the teacher to foster such "fruitful transactions" between the student-reader and the text. One way to do this is to provide a strategy in which children are invited to respond in a personal way to characters in children's literature. Fictional Role-Plays is such a strategy, in that children are asked to become the characters while their classmates ask them probing questions about their behaviors and motivations.

## Description

When reading a book with many complex characters to a group of young children, Fictional Role-Plays can help make the characters in the book come alive and through interactive questioning help children discover the relationship between what they are reading and their own lives (Cecil 1994). Use the procedure for Fictional Role-Plays as follows:

1. In collaboration with the students, decide on a piece of literature to role-play. Fairly lengthy works with many three-dimensional characters work best.

2. Assisted by the students, write a list on the chalkboard of all the characters in the book.

3. Assign pairs of children to each character.

4. Ask children to reread the story, this time to get to know their own character better.

5. Have each pair of children draw up a list of critical questions for other characters in the book. Such questions might be those that a reader longs to ask a character, or they can be posed character to

character. Also, encourage children to ask probing questions that go beyond the scope of the book.

6. After this preparation has been completed, the students are ready for the role-playing. Have each pair wear a character name tag so other class members can identify the character they wish to question, then have all sit in a circle.

7. Open the session by asking a question to a pair of characters, modeling the strategy. If the answer is offered superficially or with a simple yes or no response, then demonstrate to the children how to probe to get the character to elaborate.

8. Have the students go around the circle, asking a question of a different character each time. Encourage other children to ask follow-up questions to each question, such as "Could you tell me more about that?" or "Why did you think so?"

## Example

Sixth-grade students decided to do a fictional role-play with the story *Peter Pan*, after reading the book and watching the video in class. To start, the teacher, with the students' help, made a list of characters from the book and assigned roles to pairs of children.

| | | |
|---|---|---|
| Author | Wendy | John |
| Captain Hook | Lost boy (1) | Tinkerbell |
| Mr. Darling | Pirate (1) | Crocodile (Tick Tock) |
| Mrs. Darling | Nana (dog) | Indian Princess |
| Peter Pan | Michael | Mr. Snee |

The students reviewed the story in light of their own character and created questions they wanted to ask other characters in the book. The following day, the children sat in a circle with their name tags around their necks and asked questions.

STUDENT: Peter Pan, do you ever see Wendy anymore now that she has grown up?

PETER PAN: Yes, I stop in every once in a while to see how she's doing. She's not any fun anymore, though. She has two children of her own and she's a secretary. She's not interested in flying around anymore.

STUDENT: Pirate, what do you think your punishment might have been if you had gotten caught trying to make people walk the plank?

PIRATE: Gosh, I wasn't thinking about punishment; I was just having fun! I bet they would give me life imprisonment unless I pleaded insanity. I think I would get away with it, too, because nobody else I know does anything so cruel as making people jump into water with a crocodile. Maybe I *am* crazy!

STUDENT: Mrs. Darling, how did you feel when you first learned that your children were gone from the nursery?

MRS. DARLING: Well, I was very upset, of course.

ANOTHER STUDENT: If you were so upset about losing your children, Mrs. Darling, why didn't you call the FBI or something?

STUDENT: Peter Pan, can you explain why it is that you don't want to grow up?

PETER PAN: When I'm a child, I can do just exactly what I want to do and fly around always having fun. If I don't grow up I will never have to go out and get a job and pay bills and taxes.

## PROMPTING

### Rationale

Often when a teacher asks a question and a student has been selected to respond to it, that student will answer only part of the question, or none at all. Prompting is used when the teacher needs to clarify the question so that the student can understand it better, wants to encourage the student to amplify the response, or wants to elicit additional responses from the student. Prompting enables the teacher to verify whether the student actually has a critical understanding of the material, but also ensures that the student's sense of competence is not diminished by lack of success.

## Description

The first rule: always prompt in a positive manner. As you develop the strategy of prompting, there are many steps you can follow. Some are

1. Acknowledge the student's response.
2. If the student has not answered a question correctly, prompt.
3. Ask for clarification or elaboration.
4. Respond positively to a correct or partially correct clarification.
5. Prompt the student to restate the answer more completely or more logically. If this is successful, offer specific praise.
6. If the student is still unable to restate the answer more completely or logically, ask if another classmate can assist the student.

## Example

In this fifth-grade classroom, the students had just read Katherine Paterson's *Bridge to Terabithia*. The teacher-guided discussion, which shows the teacher prompting Evelyn, went as follows:

> TEACHER: Why did Jesse and Leslie become friends? It seemed to me very unlikely that the two would form a friendship. (*Wait time*) Evelyn?

> EVELYN: Well…they liked to race each other.

> TEACHER: Yes, they both enjoyed running and that is how they first met; exactly right! What other things did they enjoy doing together that made their friendship grow?

> EVELYN: They swung on the rope across the river.

TEACHER: OK…that's part of it. Now, what did they do when they got on the other side of the creek?

EVELYN: Well, they built Terabithia together. It was like their own special little place where they were the rulers and neat things happened. They…they both liked using their imaginations. Um…that's what Jesse liked about Leslie, the part about not feeling afraid to make stuff up.

TEACHER: Great! You really understood their friendship! Now how about going back to summarize what you discovered about the reasons for their friendship?

# CHAPTER 5

# STUDENT QUESTIONING STRATEGIES FOR PRIMARY GRADES

The most exciting times in teaching occur, many teachers would argue, when children are so interested and involved in a subject that the questions emanate from them. They are no longer just pleasing the teacher, but are asking questions of themselves, of the teacher, and of each other merely for the joy of learning.

If asking appropriate questions is difficult for teachers, it is also a lofty task for students. Beginning even in the primary grades, however, children can be taught to ask their own questions by using activities such as the ones in this chapter. The activities are also appropriate for older students as the difficulty of the content increases.

## SELF-INSTRUCTION

### Rationale

Self-Instruction helps learners become aware of their own cognitive processes through self-questioning (McNeil 1984). The assumption is that if the student can connect the use of this strategy to particular gains in understanding, he will then use the strategy when the teacher is not around. The practice of asking students to state what they are doing and why they are doing it when they are learning any new strategy is one way to help them make the connection between self-questioning and actual learning.

### Description

Self-Instruction is actually a combination of three metacognitive strategies—self-interrogation, verbal monitoring, and thinking aloud—to make learners become aware of their own thinking. A student using Self-Instruction does the following:

+ defines the problem (*What do I have to do?*)
+ focuses attention (*What is the main idea in this paragraph?*)
+ plans an action (*The main idea is a summary of the most important ideas in a piece of writing. I will look for a sentence that sums up what this paragraph is all about.*)
+ evaluates (*Have I found it yet?*)
+ encourages self (*That's all right—I'll keep trying.*)
+ revises (*Could the main idea be* more *than one sentence?*)
+ copes (*I'll try this new plan.*)

When you teach self-instructional strategies, you first model, talking aloud to the class, while demonstrating a particular reading task (drawing conclusions, determining the topic sentence, and so forth). Then, the children "rehearse" the strategy you have shown them by telling what they are doing as they are doing it (see statements and self-questions above). These rehearsals aloud are followed by silent rehearsals: children attack a reading task by using Self-Instruction independently but reporting on their strategies. Finally, students practice using the reading task on their own with a variety of other materials. The same procedure—modeling, rehearsal aloud, silent rehearsal, practice with other reading material—is carried out with other reading tasks such as finding supporting evidence for a generalization, locating specific information, or inferring mood. In every case, the components of problem definition—focus, plan of action, evaluation, encouragement, revision, and coping, as necessary—should be present.

## Example

After reading the following paragraphs, a second-grade student used Self-Instruction to choose a title for a passage about veterinarians.

What kind of person would be a good vet? It's important to do well in school, but you need more than good grades to be a good vet. You must like animals and care about helping them when they are sick.

You have to look carefully—to watch your patient's behavior to figure out what it may be feeling. And you should enjoy working out puzzles. You'll have some of the pieces: the patient's temperature, the sound of its heart and lungs, the results of blood tests, how the eyes and ears look, and how the body feels, for example. Then you have to put all the information together to figure out what is wrong.

The child proceeded as follows:

1. *He defined the problem.* "Well, I have to make a title for this passage."

2. *He focused attention.* "The title tells what the passage is going to be about."

3. *He planned an action.* "If I can think of one or two words that are found in most of the sentences in the paragraphs, that will probably be a good title."

4. *He evaluated.* "How about *I Want to Be a Vet*? No, it doesn't tell about all that stuff about puzzles. I have to think of a better one."

5. *He encouraged himself.* "That one wasn't good, but that's OK; I'll think of another one."

6. *He revised.* "The second part is all about what you have to do to be a vet. How about *Becoming a Vet*?"

7. *He coped.* "I'll look at all these sentences now and see if they go with *Becoming a Vet*."

## QUESTION-ANSWER RELATIONSHIPS (QARs)

### Rationale

The three metacognitive processes necessary for proficient reading are (1) self-knowledge (knowing one's own strengths and weaknesses in understanding text), (2) self-monitoring (awareness of whether or not comprehension is occurring), and (3) task knowledge (knowing what reading strategies are required by the particular reading material). Question-Answer Relationships, or QARs (Raphael 1982), help children discover for themselves whether the questions they are being asked are explicitly answered in the text or require more than one source of information (or divergent thinking) that is not totally based upon text information.

### Description

Through this strategy for understanding how to answer specific questions, students are taught the different tactics a reader uses to answer literal, inferential, critical, and creative questions. Specifically, the child asks himself "Where can I find an answer?", then uses the following hierarchy of questions and answers to decide.

+ *Question type 1 (literal).* Answer: "Right there." This tells the child that the answer is easy to find in the story. The exact words in the question are contained in the story.

+ *Question type 2 (inferential).* Answer: "Think and search." This tells the child that the answer can be found in the story, but he will have to put two ideas together; that is, the words used in the question may be a bit different from the words used in the story, so the answer will be a little harder to find.

+ *Question type 3 (critical).* Answer: "The author and me." The answer is in the story, but there is only one way the question can be answered—from the author's point of view. The child may think of another way to answer the question after considering the author's ideas.

✦ *Question type 4 (creative).* Answer: "On my own." The child won't find the "exact" answer to this kind of question in the story. The answer may come from his imagination or from information he already knows about the topic.

Following is an outline of how you can train children to incorporate this helpful strategy into their reading and thinking.

*First session:* Give students a passage with questions for which the question types have already been determined. Discuss with them how each question-and-answer relationship is decided. Then give them a passage for which they must determine the type of question and find the answer in the passage.

*Second session:* Provide students with longer passages of several paragraphs and with up to eight questions per passage. Allow students to discuss the questions in small cooperative groups with your guidance.

*Third session:* Give students entire stories to read, divided into four sections. Provide eight questions, two from each category, for each section.

*Fourth session:* Offer material from other curricular materials (for example, science and social studies) accompanied by two or three questions for each QAR category. Instruct students to read the passage, respond to each question by identifying the QAR, and then discuss the answer.

## Example

After reading an excerpt from C. J. Nader's *Pegasus the Winged Horse*, these third-graders used QARs to help them answer the four categories of questions.

> Long ago in Ancient Greece, there was a very special horse called Pegasus. He was special because he could fly. Pegasus had great snowy wings that lifted him right into the clouds. Sometimes he played games in the clouds, gliding from one to another like a big white bird.

Everyone on earth loved Pegasus because he was such a beautiful and gentle horse. And he was a favorite, too, with the gods and goddesses who lived high on Mount Olympus.

TEACHER: What made Pegasus special?

DION: Right there. He was special because he could fly.

TEACHER: What did Pegasus do for fun?

DION: Think and search, because it doesn't use those words exactly. He played games in the clouds.

TEACHER: Do you think Pegasus was very popular? Why?

DION: Think and search. I would say he was very popular because it says here that everyone on earth loved him and he was also a favorite with the gods and goddesses.

TEACHER: Why do you think everyone liked Pegasus so much?

JENNIFER: Think and search. It says that Pegasus was a beautiful and gentle horse. That's probably why everyone loved him so much.

SIM: I think it's author and me. Being beautiful and gentle may have been part of it, but probably they loved him too because it was so unusual to see a horse that could fly.

TEACHER: Was he part of the earth or part of the sky?

DION: Author and me. People on earth loved him and so did the gods and goddesses, but it's not really clear whether he was *part* of one or the other. I think he was probably more part of the sky because he enjoyed flying so much.

TEACHER: Would you like to own a horse who could fly? Why or why not?

JENNIFER: On my own. This is definitely just my own opinion. I would love to have a winged horse that I could fly all over the world with, especially a pretty, gentle one.

SIM: Yeah, it's on my own. Because I have a different opinion. I really love horses, but I would prefer one who would just be normal and gallop around places. People would stare at you too much if you had a flying horse.

## BASAL READER PREDICTION STRATEGY

### Rationale

When students make predictions about what something is about prior to reading, they have set their own purpose—they will read to see if their predictions are supported in the passage. Moreover, when students share and discuss their predictions, friendly arguments about whose predictions are correct often follow, adding even more impetus to the reading task (Tierney, Readence & Dishner 1985). Buckley (1986) avows that writing can be used to help students develop elaborate predictions about the basal stories they are about to read.

### Description

Pair students or divide the class into small groups, then do the following (basal reader stories or stories from trade books may be used):

1. Have the partners or members of the group leaf through all the illustrations in the story in order. Then have each partner or group member carefully describe what is happening in one of the illustrations. After each illustration is described, have the next student in the rotation predict aloud what will happen in that part of the story.

2. After all the illustrations in the story have been discussed, have each child write his own story predicting what will happen in the story, according to what was described in the illustrations.

3. Have partners or group members share their stories and discuss their opinion about the accuracy of each other's predictions.

4. Have the partners or group members take turns reading the story aloud or silently to check their predictions.

5. Have the partners or group members compare the story with their predictive stories and discuss who came closest to the actual story line.

### Example

A pair of second-grade readers made predictions, then read *Puss in Boots*. This is what happened. (Note: The process continued until all the illustrations had been discussed.)

1. LEON: In the first picture it shows three men and one of them has a cat in his arms. It looks like it is his cat and he loves it a lot.

   MICAH: I think the other two men are going to try to take the cat away from the man. *(Pauses)* My turn for the next picture. This is the same man 'cause he has the same clothes on, but he looks younger, like a boy. The cat is talking to him and he looks surprised.

   LEON: I think the cat is telling the boy that he will take care of him.

2. Leon and Micah wrote the following predictive stories based upon the discussions and predictions they made for each illustration:

   **Micah's Story**
   The cat who can talk gets all dressed up in fancy clothes. He meets a bad man and then a lion and a mouse. The cat makes the boy who owns him rich. He becomes a king and he still keeps his cat.

   **Leon's Story**
   The boy is afraid of his cat because he can talk. He tries to get rid of him. The cat puts on a costume and goes in the woods. He goes to see the king. The king tells him to bring the boy back, so he does.

3. Leon and Micah shared their written stories with each other. Micah argued intensely that the boy still loved the cat; Leon didn't think so but was less sure. Both agreed it is not a true story.

4. The two children read *Puss in Boots*.

5. The two then had the following discussion:

LEON: Neither one of us got it that the cat could change himself into other animals.

MICAH: Yeah, but I was right about the boy still caring for the cat. The cat was a *good* cat and I said that.

LEON: But I was right about the king. He [the cat] went to see the king. He was trying to get money for his master, who was poor.

MICAH: You were right in some ways, I was right in some ways.

## SCHEMA-GENERAL QUESTIONS

### Rationale

Many sets of questions in instructional materials appear to interfere with—rather than enhance—comprehension. That is, the questions suggested in the teachers' manuals are not likely to help children organize and internalize the key ideas. Therefore, teachers should teach children to ask their own questions based upon the logical organization of events and ideas of central importance to the story and their connections, and introduce them to story grammars.

### Description

Harry Singer and Dan Donlon (1982) developed a strategy called Schema-General Questions, to connect the relationships in narrative (story) structure. With this strategy, students decide upon the starting point of the story and then list in summary form the major events and ideas that make up the plot and the links between events, or the gist of the story. Implied ideas that are part of the story but are not directly stated are included. Finally, children ask questions to glean information that matches the progression of ideas and events.

Specifically, children are taught to ask themselves questions about the following, in oral or written format: (1) the main character, (2) the goal, (3) the problem, (4) the resolution, and (5) the theme.

1. *The main character*
   + Who is the main character?
   + What does the character do?
   + What have I learned about the character from what he or she has done?

2. *The goal*
   + What does the main character want?
   + What have I learned about the main character after discovering his or her goal?
   + What does the main character do to reach his or her goal?
   + What have I learned about the main character from what that character has done?

3. *The problem*
   + What is the first problem that the main character has?
   + What does the main character do about it?
   + How does the main character change as a result of the problem?
   + What does this tell me about the main character?

4. *The resolution*
   + Does the main character get what she or he wants?
   + What has helped the character *most:* Forces within that character's control? Forces beyond that character's control? Name them.

5. *The theme*
   + What does the story basically tell about?
   + a struggle with self
   + a struggle with nature
   + a struggle with others

**Example**

Using this strategy, a third-grade class logically organized the events and ideas in Brian Birchall's *Kahu, the Cautious Kiwi*. Following is one student's written summary of the story, using Singer and Donlon's format:

1. *The main character.* Kahu, the kiwi, is the main character. A kiwi is a very shy kind of bird who lives in New Zealand. Kahu is too big to live with his parents anymore, so he goes off to live by himself in a rimu tree. I learned about Kahu that he was very brave to go out on his own and his growing up.

2. *The goal.* Kahu just wants to live a peaceful life sleeping all day and looking for worms and grubs all night. I learned that kiwis have very simple lives. He doesn't really want much except to be left alone. It's not really a goal, but that's what he tries to do just by going about his life.

3. *The problem.* A pig hunter and his dogs come along and the dogs chased Kahu. He ran into the bush to get away and his foot got caught in a trap. A wild cat tried to attack Kahu, but Kahu hit the cat's face with his other claw. Kahu is changed because he's frightened and all alone. I bet he wishes he hadn't left his family.

4. *The resolution.* Kahu got the peaceful life he wanted but not right away. First a boy comes along and gets Kahu out of the trap. He takes Kahu home with him and they become friends. He helps his leg get well. He follows the boy around. He follows him to school and the teacher sees him. The teacher says kiwis are protected birds and the boy should take him back to the bush. So forces beyond Kahu's control got Kahu what he wanted, because the boy let him go in the bush and he was really happy.

5. *The theme.* This story told mostly about a struggle of a kiwi against the world, because he would have been happy in nature, but man-made things like a trap caused him to have big problems.

---

## Schema-General Questions

**Name** _____ **Date** _____

**Book Title** _____

Using the questions you have learned to ask yourself,
write a summary of the book under the following headings.


The Main Character


The Goal


The Problem


The Resolution


The Theme

*Figure 12. Schema-General Questions*

# CHAPTER 6

# STUDENT QUESTIONING STRATEGIES FOR INTERMEDIATE GRADES

T he cruxes of critical thinking are reflection and the ability to consider a host of possible alternatives. As children move into the intermediate grades they are ready to experience a greater degree of independence in their thinking. This is the time to encourage them to ask their own thoughtful questions about content as they begin to make sense of what they read in fresh and original ways.

## DYAD READING

### Rationale

Paired oral reading experiences have two advantages: (1) large numbers of children can practice reading at the same time; and (2) both children in each pair are actively involved at all times, either as reader or listener. With Dyad Reading, or two-person reading, a third advantage is added: one child must purposefully listen to the other child, then summarize what that child has said. The reader then asks the person who summarized a critical question from the text. Children quickly learn to ask each other higher-level questions rather than those requiring simple yes or no answers.

### Description

Dyad Reading is a form of reciprocal oral reading that has the added dimension of increasing important critical-thinking skills through summarizing and questioning. You can teach the strategy using the following format:

1. Select two children and have one read a paragraph aloud. (With younger children, this can be reduced to one sentence.)

2. As that child reads, have the other child listen and then summarize (oral or written) what was in the paragraph. (For variation, the second child may draw what was read, then describe the picture.)

3. Have the reader ask the listener critical-thinking questions.

4. Encourage the children to discuss the answers and, where there is disagreement, have them refer back to the paragraph to support their answers.

5. Have the children rotate the process.

When you feel the children are ready to practice this strategy independently, divide the class into pairs or threesomes. (In a threesome, a child who is a limited-English speaker or a nonreader can get the gist of the passage by listening to it being read first, then hearing it being summarized.)

**Example**

Three fifth-grade children were reading Nina Bawden's *The Outside Child*. It is about a young girl who finds out she has a half brother and sister.

Lila read the following paragraph aloud:

> It was easier talking to Plato's mother than I would have expected. She had asked a question occasionally, but until she thought of Pandora she had listened in silence, sitting on the end of the couch. She had made me lie down on it to "rest" as if I were an invalid. Plato was sitting on the floor, back against the wall, hugging his knees and listening with a broody expression. I had told them what had actually happened. What I hadn't told them was how I had felt when Amy had started to scream. That once ages ago I must have done something dreadfully wicked. It seemed too shameful to mention (Bawden: 141).

Samantha summarized the paragraph: "Jane was worried about talking to Plato's mother, but it's no big deal. She turns out to be a pretty good listener. She feels really ashamed of what she is telling them and she's wondering what Plato's reaction will be."

The third child, Rachel, spoke little English, but was able to quickly sketch her understanding of the paragraph, augmented by Samantha's summary. She shared her picture with Lila and Samantha.

Lila, after asking if she could add to the summary, said: "Jane also was lying down because Plato's mother kept treating her like an invalid." She then asked Samantha: "What do you think Jane was expecting Plato's mother to do when she heard her story? If it was easier than she thought, what do you think she expected to have happened?"

"I think she expected Plato's mother to be shocked," Samantha replied.

"Why would she have been shocked?" Lila asked. "She told them what happened, but not everything. The bad parts she left out. See…it says 'What I hadn't told them was how I felt when Amy had started to scream…It seemed too shameful to mention.'"

## I-SEARCH

### Rationale

Searching for information about a topic of special interest and then connecting the ideas from that search to others is an adventure in learning. The I-Search strategy helps children search for critical information, but also to realize that there is a personal story behind every research paper (even though the pronoun *I* is rarely used in such writing). The strategy helps children develop research skills while offering them the experience of telling the background story about the search for information.

### Description

Freedman (1986) suggests teaching children to use the I-Search in three phases: (1) problem identification, (2) information quest, and (3) writing the paper.

1.  *Problem identification.* With the students, brainstorm a list of topics in which they are interested. When they have chosen their favorite from among these topics, have them, as a group, write statements about the topic, followed by a list of questions they have about the topic.

2.  *Information quest.* Model for students how they can get the information they need to answer their questions, using library references, trade books, or by interviewing resource people.

3.  *Writing the paper.* Give children a specific format to follow, which requires them to ask themselves three key questions about the research task:

    ✦ What do I want to know? (*statement of the problem*)
    ✦ How will I find the information I need? (*procedures*)
    ✦ What did I find out? (*summary*)

After introducing this activity to the class, the strategy can best be implemented with individual students or in small cooperative groups. Write topic suggestions on the chalkboard, and put any information the children already have about the topic in a separate column. Next, provide each student or group with an I-Search activity sheet (see Blackline Master, page 159).

By asking their own questions, children are introduced to the fundamentals of research (including the preparation of bibliographies) through this experience. With the I-Search sheet providing the essential format for a research paper, the writer's task is then to flesh out the sections and combine them into a complete report. An I-Search activity sheet reminds children of the procedures they must follow and the critical questions they must ask themselves (see figure 13).

### Example

Two students, working as partners, used the I-Search strategy to learn about Hispanics.

1.  *What do I want to know?* The children, both Hispanic, brain-

| **I-Search** |
|---|

**Name** _Juan and Michael_         **Date** _Feb. 16_

**Question** _How have Hispanics contributed to American life?_

| **What do I already know?** | **Information:** Hispanics contribute to our country in many ways. We celebrate Cinco de Mayo because of them and they speak Spanish. We have lots of Mexican restaurants. | |
|---|---|---|
| **How do I find the information I need?** | **Sources:** Franco, John. Hispano-American Contributes to American Life. Benefic Press, 1990. | **What the Sources Said:** There have been educators, scientists, businessmen, actors, entertainers, athletes, physicians, government officials, and labor leaders that were famous. |
| | Current Biography Yearbook. H.W. Wilson Company, 1990. | Many Hispanics were prejudiced against and grew up poor. It was hard for them to succeed but some worked hard and made it. |
| **What did I discover?** | 1. Hispanics are important in every part of American society. <br> 2. Some Hispanics are very poor and have a hard life. They experience lots of prejudice. Not everyone appreciates what they have to offer. <br> 3. Hispanics have contributed to every part of our lives: they have been doctors, lawyers, scientists, government officials, entertainers, actors, and athletes. | |

*Figure 13. I-Search Activity Sheet*

stormed, decided on a topic to investigate, then formed the question "How have Hispanics contributed to American life?" They wrote this at the top of their activity sheet.

They discussed, then wrote down in the information section, all the things they could think of that they already knew about their topic and any questions they had.

2. *How do I find the information I need?* With teacher guidance, the children found two resources: *Hispanic American Contributors to American Life,* a trade book, and a reference book, *Current Biography.* They wrote down the bibliographic information as well as the information that they got from these sources.

3. *What did I find out?* The students summarized the results of their investigation, and, where necessary, revised statements they had made prior to doing the research. In this case, they had a startling —and welcome—revelation when they discovered their heritage was a good deal more rich than just tacos and Cinco de Mayo, as they had previously thought.

## QUESTION GENERATING

### Rationale

Carefully modeled by competent teachers, Question Generating may be the most useful strategy of all for promoting the construction of meaning before, during, and after reading. The strategy may have little value, however, if it is not well taught (Pressley et al. 1990).

### Description

Question Generating (Cooper 1993) is a strategy to help children improve their ability to construct meaning by having them generate their own questions about text, then finding the answers through reading. The process involves showing children how to generate key questions so they assimilate important information as they read. To do this, children need to learn to internalize the following steps as they read:

1. *Skim the material to be read.*
   - ✦ Look at the cover and illustrations.
   - ✦ Read titles and subtitles.
   - ✦ Read the introduction and summary.

2. *Ask a question about the topic.*
   - ✦ Make the title into a question.
   - ✦ Write it down.

3. *Read the passage to find answers to the question.*
   - ✦ Write down the answer.
   - ✦ Decide if the question was a good critical question.
   - ✦ Revise the question, if necessary.

4. *Ask another question about the topic.*
   - ✦ Decide if this question can be answered from the reading.
   - ✦ Write down the question.

5. *Read more of the passage to find answers to the question and continue to think of questions they have as they read.*
   - ✦ Write down their questions.
   - ✦ Write down their answers.

6. *Save questions that cannot be answered through the passage for research to do at a later time.*

## Example

A fourth-grade student used the Question Generating strategy to construct meaning of the text "Young Man with a Mission: Albert Schweitzer."

1. *Skim the material.* The student skimmed the piece, looking at the illustrations and reading the first paragraph (some expository text has no introduction or summary).

2. *Ask a question about the topic.* She wrote down this question: "What was Albert Schweitzer's mission?"

3. *Read the passage to answer your questions.* The student read the passage and wrote the following answer to her question: "Albert

Schweitzer's *mission* was to become a medical missionary in Africa and to help the people there." She then considered whether or not this was a good critical question. She decided it was, as most of the passage concerned Schweitzer's medical mission in Africa.

4. *Ask another question about the topic.* The student thought about what she had read so far, then wrote: "Did Schweitzer ever regret his decision to become a medical missionary?"

5. *Read more of the passage to find the answers to your question.* She read on and her question was soon answered. She wrote: "Albert Schweitzer had made up his mind and nothing could change it. He did not have enough money to go to the university and they tried to persuade him to give up his dream. His wife got sick and had to go and live in Switzerland and he could only see her once in a while. But still he loved what he was doing and was very successful at healing lots of people. No, I don't think he ever regretted it."

6. *Save questions that cannot be answered through the passage for research to do at a later time.* The student, fascinated by Albert Schweitzer, wrote down the following questions:

   - Is Dr. Schweitzer's hospital still running in Lambarene?
   - How did he die?
   - Did the people in Africa ever wonder why a white man would help them that way?
   - Did he ever get any bad diseases?
   - Did he ever win any awards for his courage?

## COGNITIVE STRATEGY INSTRUCTION IN WRITING (CSIW)

### Rationale

A strategy that has proven effective in helping students do expository writing is the Cognitive Strategy Instruction in Writing (CSIW) (Raphael & Englebert 1990). Incorporating a writing strategy with reading can improve students' ability to do expository writing, help them understand different organizational structures, and improve their ability to construct their own meaning through self-questioning (Konapale, S.H. Martin & M.A. Martin 1990).

## Description

CSIW has been used with intermediate-grade students to help them write and read expository material, by having them ask their own questions. The strategy is based upon four principles: (1) text analysis, (2) modeling, (3) guided practice, and (4) independent writing.

1.  *Text analysis.* Model for the students how to analyze a piece of writing in terms of the text structure—sequence, problem/solution, enumeration, comparison, description, or cause/effect. For the demonstration, use something you have written or select a passage from a book.

2.  *Modeling.* Select a topic that fits with a specific organizational structure for writing, then use a Think Sheet to model how you plan and organize a piece of writing (see Blackline Master, page 160). The following questions are useful:

    + What is my topic?
    + Who am I writing for?
    + What do I already know about the topic?
    + Where can I get more information?
    + What organizational structure makes sense?
    + What are some beginning ideas?
    + What are some ending ideas?

3.  *Guided practice.* Have the students select their own topics and write their own papers, soliciting guidance from you as necessary.

4.  *Independent writing.* After plenty of guided practice using several different organizational structures, give each student a Think Sheet. Have them plan and organize their own writing independently. Encourage them to combine several structures, as writers often do.

---

**CSIW**

---

**Name** _Randy H._       **Date** _January 18_

**Topic** _Bathing a dog_

**What** is my topic?

Giving your dog a bath.

**Who** am I writing for?

My family, teacher, and classmates will read this.

**What** do I already know about this topic?

I give my dog a bath every week and I'm really good at it, but most people aren't. Most dogs hate to take a bath.

**Where** can I get more information on this topic?

In the library is a magazine called Pet Care. I will also look for other library books about dogs and pets.

**What** organizational structure should I use?

You have to do everything in the right order, so I think I should use sequence.

**What** are some beginning ideas?

Lots of dogs like mine don't like to get baths, so you have to bribe them. I will talk about how I bribe Laddie with a toy mouse or a dog bone.

**What** are some ending ideas?

How my dog looks as good as new afterwards and you feel proud and the dog does too.

---

*Figure 14. CSIW Think Sheet*

## Example

A fourth-grade boy used the CSIW strategy to write an expository piece about bathing his dog (see figure 14). (This was his first attempt using CSIW on his own.)

# METACOGNITIVE STRATEGY

## Rationale

When children read in school, they need to be guided in developing metacognitive, or self-monitoring, strategies so that these important skills become an internalized part of their normal reading behavior. Metacognitive strategies give readers a sense of how much or how little they are bringing to the reading task, what the task is, and what is expected of them. Such strategies help readers know when and if their comprehension is failing them and what they should do to correct the situation.

## Description

The School District of Philadelphia developed a metacognitive strategy through the MERIT Chapter 2 Project (1986) that significantly helped children monitor their own comprehension. The proponents explain that when a reader is reading fluently with adequate comprehension, he is said to be "c-l-i-c-k-i-n-g a-l-o-n-g." But when something comes along that is not understood—an unfamiliar word, reference, or idea—the reader hits a "c-l-u-n-k." A proficient reader usually realizes that a problem has been encountered and takes steps to correct it. This strategy delineates the seven steps needed to correct a problem in comprehension, adapted here to a self-questioning format.

1. *Am I reading too fast?* Students need to be taught that a social studies textbook, for example, should not be read at the same speed as a mystery story. Students need, therefore, to first question the rate at which they are trying to read the material to see if they should be reading at a more careful rate.

2. *Will the author explain the "clunk" if I continue reading?* Often a word, idea, or reference will be explained satisfactorily if the reader is patient and waits for the meaning to be cleared up through the context or by the addition of new information.

3. *Should I reread what I just read?* Often a passage makes more sense to the reader a second time; sometimes, a word that has been decoded incorrectly or omitted is corrected upon rereading.

4. *Should I study the diagrams, maps, charts, graphs, or other aids the text has provided?* Much information is provided in diagrams in expository material and children need to learn to study these important additions to texts.

5. *Can I look up an unfamiliar word or term in the glossary, the dictionary, or in my textbook?* When vocabulary is the issue, children need to accept their lack of knowledge and know what they can do to rectify it.

6. *Should I talk to another classmate about this problem or question?* In a child-centered classroom, children feel free to try to straighten out the comprehension barrier through discussion with a trusted friend. Often talking through a comprehension problem helps the child work it out.

7. *Could the teacher help with this problem?* Because the essence of positive metacognitive self-questioning skills is to help the child become an independent thinker, this final step is a *last resort*. But if the child is aware that he is not comprehending, this is a good strategy. After exhausting all other resources, you or another adult can often shed some light on what the possible problem might be.

## Example

A sixth-grade boy was reading a passage called "Catalonia, a Modern Country with Centuries of Tradition." The transcript of the boy's questions and answers to himself show how the child used Metacognitive Strategy to work out a comprehension problem.

The child read:

> Catalonia, a country in Spain with its own culture, language,
> and identity, has its Patron Saint's day, Sant Jordi, on April 23.
> And on this day the rose and the book become part of
> Catalonia itself.

The boy was confused. "I don't understand. How are a rose and a book 'part of Catalonia?' What does that mean?" He began to go through his hierarchy of questions in the Metacognitive Strategy:

1. "Am I reading too fast? Maybe I am. This is about social studies and I know I am supposed to slow down for work-type reading. I'll slow down a little, but I don't think that's the problem."

2. "Will the author explain the "clunk" if I continue reading? Okay, I'll try that and see." He read the next sentence.

   > The rose represents coexistence, affection, and community spirit,
   > and the book stands for culture and love of language.

   "Oh, I get it. The book and the rose are like symbols for things. The people of the country use them to mean what they feel about their country. But now I am confused by the word *coexistence*. I don't know what that means."

3. "Should I reread what I just read? I reread it and I still don't understand that word, but I'm more sure that I was right about the rose and book being symbols for other things. I'm just not sure of what the rose is a symbol for."

4. "Should I study the diagrams, maps, charts, graphs, or other aids the text has provided? There is a map here and it shows me that Catalonia is a little part of Spain and that Barcelona is a city that is in it. That helps, but it doesn't tell me everything about this word, I don't think."

5. "Can I look up an unfamiliar word or term in the glossary, the dictionary, or in my textbook? This book doesn't have a glossary

and I can't find an answer in my textbook. I'll look it up in my dictionary. It says that coexistence means 'existing together or at the same time.' I still don't understand what it means that the rose represents 'existing together.'"

6. "Should I talk to a classmate about this problem or question? I'll try that." (He read the passage aloud to his friend, Tony, and asked him what he thought it meant.) "Tony said he thinks it's talking about the people of Catalonia existing together in peace, kind of like English people and French people in Canada live together, or coexist. I think Tony is right—that makes sense to me."

At this point, the child had no need to consult the teacher, and was able to complete the passage successfully, continuing to ask himself questions about his construction of meaning of the passage.

## SURVEY, QUESTION, READ, RECITE, AND REVIEW (SQ3R)

### Rationale

Study methods are strategies that students can learn to help them study written material in a way that enhances comprehension through self-questioning and answering. Such strategies are student-directed, rather than teacher-directed, and are implemented to help students remember content material better than they would by simply reading the material.

### Description

Probably the best-known study method is Robinson's SQ3R method. SQ3R is an acronym for the five steps: Survey, **Q**uestion, **R**ead, **R**ecite, and **R**eview (Robinson 1961). If you take the time in class to show students how to go through the various steps and hold group practice sessions before the students perform the steps independently, the steps will begin to become ingrained in the students' minds.

1. *Survey.* Select a passage, then, with the students, survey the selection, reading aloud the chapter titles and main headings, introductory and summary paragraphs, and inspecting and discussing any visual aids such as maps, graphs, or illustrations. Explain that this initial survey provides a framework for organizing the facts that will later be derived from the reading.

2. *Question.* Show the children how to formulate questions from chapter headings, main headings, and titles. These questions, which provide a good purpose for reading, should be answered in the next section. Encourage children to generate other questions, and add ones that you expect the children might be able to answer from the reading.

3. *Read.* With the children, read the selection to find answers to the questions that have been formulated. You may want to make brief notes on the chalkboard to model behavior the children can follow. (This is purposeful reading, and making brief notes may be helpful.)

4. *Recite.* Have the children try to answer each of the questions formulated earlier, without looking at the passage.

5. *Review.* With the children, reread the passage to verify or correct your recited answers, to make sure you have the main points of the selection in mind, and to help you understand the relationships between the various points.

**Example**

A fourth-grade class was preparing to read a chapter in social studies entitled, "The Westward Movement." Guided by their teacher, they went through the steps in SQ3R.

1. *Survey.* The students looked over the chapter briefly and then read the title, the main heading, the introduction, and the summary together.

2. *Question.* The children turned the chapter title "The Westward Movement" into the question "What was the Westward Movement?" The teacher listed other questions from headings and subheadings on the chalkboard.

   + When did the Westward Movement happen?
   + Why did it take place?
   + Where did they go?
   + Who was involved?
   + What was it like to go westward?

3. *Read.* The children read the selection to find answers to their questions.

4. *Recite.* Without looking at the chapter, the children answered the questions aloud. Because they had asked their own questions, they found the answers easier to remember.

5. *Review.* There was a difference of opinion in response to "Why did the westward movement take place?" One child believed it was to search for a better life; another was certain it was to find gold. The students went back to the text to settle the disagreement (they were both correct). Each child supported his answer by reading the information from the text.

## Related Information

Newspapers provide excellent vehicles through which to practice this kind of questioning, but the steps followed vary slightly from that in SQ3R. After choosing an article of interest, have the child follow these six steps (Cecil 1994):

1. Skim the article quickly.

2. List four questions you have about the article.

3. Read the article to find answers to your questions.

4. Rewrite the article, answering the questions.

5. Recite from memory all you have learned from the article.

6. List any questions you still have about the subject.

# CHAPTER 7

# QUESTIONS ACROSS THE CURRICULUM

I n far too many classrooms, subjects like language arts and science are isolated into separate disciplines that promote neither depth of understanding nor connections with other subjects. Learning is assumed to take place primarily through one vehicle—the textbook—and this is frequently *not* read by the students (Armbruster 1991a), but read aloud by the teacher, or the information from it simply told to the students. By contrast, learning across the curriculum is interactive, inviting all children to access knowledge through a variety of problem-solving experiences that can best be tied together through effective questioning strategies.

All the ideas and principles presented in this book apply as we now begin to think about questioning across the curricular areas of math, science, social studies, and art appreciation. Examples of questioning strategies introduced in the previous four chapters, as well as new ones, are presented as they are applied and connected in a variety of content areas.

## QUESTIONING IN MATHEMATICS

Questioning can help teachers connect mathematics to the rest of the curricular areas, for the goals of mathematics are remarkably similar to those of other disciplines, both cognitively and affectively. Through these goals learners develop (Hyde & Bizar 1989)

+ knowledge of math and concepts in related areas
+ an ability to problem solve, think critically, and monitor one's own thinking
+ confidence and positive attitudes about self

Let's see how three teachers in three different classrooms used questioning techniques to achieve these goals.

### VIGNETTE 1, GRADE 6.
### INTEGRATION: MATH/ORAL LANGUAGE

TEACHER: I'm going to ask you a question for which we won't be able to get an exact answer, but I want to see if we can come close. How many golf balls do you think will fit in this suitcase? (*The teacher allows the children to examine the suitcase and the golf ball.*)

RANDY: Do you want us to just guess? I guess there would be room for 300!

TEACHER: Thanks for your response, Randy, you may be right but does anyone have any idea how we could be more sure of our answer? (*Pauses, then calls on Jessica.*)

JESSICA: Could we fill up the suitcase with golf balls and find out? Then we would know for sure, I think.

TEACHER: That is one sure way, Jessica, but I have only one golf ball. Any other ideas? (*Pauses*) José?

JOSÉ: How about if we measure the golf ball and the suitcase?

JESSICA: Yes, let's do that!

(*The teacher selects three children to measure the golf ball and three to measure the suitcase.*)

JOSÉ (*for the suitcase group*): The suitcase is twenty-four inches wide and thirty inches long and eight inches high.

RANDY (*for the golf ball group*): If the ball was square, it would be about one inch by one inch.

TEACHER: So...can anyone tell me approximately how many golf balls will fit in that suitcase? (*Pauses, then, realizing the children may have forgotten how to solve the problem of finding cubic inches, prompts.*) If the suitcase is thirty inches by twenty-four inches by eight inches, can anyone estimate what the answer to this would be by multiplying the three numbers together? (*Jessica begins to compute using paper and pencil.*) Remember—we are not looking for an exact answer, just an approximation. (*Prompts*) What numbers might you use to estimate if you wanted to do the problem in your head?

JESSICA: Thirty by twenty by ten? Is that right, to round 'em off? (*The teacher smiles and nods.*) About 6000 golf balls. Wow—6000 golf balls, more or less, would fit in that suitcase.

RANDY: I was way off. The way we thought about it was way better than guessing!

## VIGNETTE 2, GRADE 5.
## INTEGRATION: MATH/ORAL LANGUAGE/LISTENING

In this classroom, the teacher used a Think Aloud strategy to provide "beginning thinkers" with a way to observe *expert thinking,* usually hidden from their view.

TEACHER: What do I do when I face a problem like this—4/6 + 2/3? I know how to add fractions when the denominator is the same, like 5/6 + 1/6, but I have no general procedure for adding them when the denominators are different, as in this problem. Probably the best thing to do for the time being is to look at some simple examples and see if I can get a clue about how this is done. Okay, here's an example: 3/4 + 1/8. What they do is make both of the denominators the same by going 3/4 = 6/8. Looking at this for a while tells me that 8 is twice as much as 4 (*Pauses to let all learners follow her thinking*), and—hey—6 is twice as much as 3. I think I will try that with my problem. Does someone want to help me with my hunch? (*Pauses*) Nuri?

NURI: You can make both fractions the same by making 2/3 into a fraction with 6 at the bottom. You say 2/3 = ?/6 and then you say 6 is twice as much as 3, so what is twice as much as 2? The answer is 4! So 2/3 = 4/6.

TEACHER: Good thinking, Nuri! Now the problem is just like the ones I already know about when I add fractions when they're the same: 4/6 + 4/6 = 8/6. Does anyone want to add their thoughts to mine?

VIGNETTE 3, GRADE 1.
INTEGRATION: MATH/ORAL LANGUAGE

The teacher in this primary classroom provided an integration of linguistic, conceptual, and mathematical experiences for her young learners as she structured their play with attribute blocks of varying colors, sizes, and shapes.

TEACHER (*To children who are seated in small groups with one bag of blocks per group*): Can anyone think of a way we could group these blocks? (*Pauses*) Cary, Chelsea, and Ben?

CARY: I pulled out all the red pieces. See?

TEACHER: All the red pieces. That is a way to group the blocks. Chelsea?

CHELSEA: I got all the blue pieces.

TEACHER: Yes, Chelsea, you sorted them in the same way Cary did—by color. Can you think of another way to group them, Chelsea?

CHELSEA: Ummm, now I got all the circles together. (*The teacher nods and looks at Ben.*)

BEN: These blocks are all big and these ones are all little.

TEACHER: Yes, Ben. Does everyone see that Ben has grouped his blocks according to their size? That is another way to group the blocks. Anything else? Can anyone use *two* ways to group the blocks? (*Prompts*) For example, can anyone use size and color? Ben and Chelsea?

BEN: See, these are little and blue!

TEACHER: Yes, very good! They are all alike in two ways: they have the same size and the same color. Chelsea?

CHELSEA: Mine are all green and they are all small.

TEACHER: Chelsea also grouped the blocks by size and color, but a different size and a different color.

## QUESTIONING IN SCIENCE

Anderson and Smith (1987) suggest that teachers ask children carefully crafted questions to elicit explanations of specific phenomena. To avoid asking only factual questions, they recommend that questions be used for the following purposes:

+ to assess and challenge students' misconceptions about scientific principles
+ to assess students' understanding of new scientific concepts
+ to stimulate students to use and apply scientific concepts to other curricular areas and in their everyday lives

VIGNETTE 4, GRADE 2.
INTEGRATION: SCIENCE/MATH (MEASURING)/ORAL LANGUAGE/WRITING

In the following second-grade class, the teacher helped the children become more structured and systematic in their inquiry. The children experimented with five different substances: sugar, baking soda, "oobleck" (cornstarch), salt, and flour. The teacher provided clear plastic glasses. Each glass held about eight ounces (250 ml) of water, which had been cooled to room temperature. Each was then placed on a sheet of paper on which was printed the name of the substance to be added. Children worked in small groups of three, each with the oobleck and two other substances.

One child in each group measured a quarter teaspoon (1 ml) of one substance and then sprinkled it into the glass. Another child in the group counted to thirty, after which the first child stirred the water gently with a spoon. A third child wrote down observations when the water stopped moving. This process was repeated with all substances, with careful observations noted each time.

The following discussion took place after the above processes were completed.

TEACHER: What happened when you put the baking soda in the water?

TONYA: It disappeared. Quickly.

TEACHER: Why do you think so? What was happening?

TONYA: It mixed with the water.

JARED: It happened every time we added it. Sugar goes away in water.

TEACHER: What about the baking soda. What happened with it?

GREG: It went away in the water every time, too.

TONYA: Ours didn't, not like the sugar.

TEACHER: Okay. What did the rest of you find with the baking soda? Linda? Beth? Nuri? (*Pauses*)

LINDA: It mixed right up quickly every single time.

BETH: Ours did too.

NURI: It disappeared faster than the sugar.

TEACHER: Okay, in general, then, we can say that the sugar mixed with the water or *dissolved* in it. (*Writes* dissolved *on the chalkboard.*) What about the salt? (*Pauses*) Nuri?

NURI: It went away—it dissolved right away—but the water was, like, all white.

TONYA: Yeah, it never went away and every time we added more it was whiter.

JARED: Some salt pieces even dropped on the bottom.

BETH: Yes, that happened to ours, too.

TEACHER: So, can anyone make a statement about sugar and baking soda compared to salt?

LINDA: Sugar and soda dissolve better than salt does.

TEACHER: Thumbs up if you agree with Linda's statement. (*Pauses*) I see you all agree. What happened with the flour? Jared?

JARED: It got all cloudy. The water was all murky. And then it just sank to the bottom.

TEACHER: Murky is a good word! Did anyone observe anything different from that happening?

LINDA: Flour didn't mix at all with the water.

BETH: It mixed up, but it didn't go away. It didn't dissolve.

TEACHER: Any statements you care to make about the flour compared to the baking soda, salt, or sugar? (*Pauses*) Tonya? Jared? Linda?

TONYA: The flour was slower mixing up than the salt, and sugar is fastest.

LINDA: Baking soda dissolves as good as sugar.

JARED: And salt is better than flour, but doesn't really dissolve.

TEACHER: Good observations! Now, what was happening with the oobleck?

LINDA: The oobleck never went away either. The oobleck doesn't dissolve, just like the flour doesn't.

TONYA: But it did faster with ours than the flour.

TEACHER: How many people found that the oobleck was different from the flour? (*Pauses*)

NURI: It went like this: Sugar and baking soda dissolved totally, salt mixed up a little bit, but made the water cloudy and didn't dissolve, and then the flour and the oobleck kept getting glumpier and glumpier in the water.

### VIGNETTE 5, GRADE 1.
### INTEGRATION: SCIENCE/ECOLOGY/READING/ SOCIAL STUDIES

This first-grade social studies teacher began her lesson on trees with a K-W-L[1] (Ogle 1986). The questions in each of the categories resulted in the following responses from the children, which the teacher listed on the chalkboard:

What do you know about trees?

+ They have leaves.
+ Some shed their leaves, some don't.
+ They give us shade.
+ Animals live in them.
+ We get wood from them.
+ You can climb them.
+ They give us fruit.
+ Some have flowers.

What would you like to know about trees?

+ How long do they live?
+ How can we protect them?
+ How can we take care of them?
+ If you cut them down, do they grow back?
+ What kills trees?

At this point, the teacher read the children *Someday a Tree,* by Eve Bunting, a story about a little girl who tells why an oak tree is impor-

---

1. K-W-L is an abbreviation for What I **K**now; What I **W**ant to Know; What I **L**earned

tant to her. This particular tree is dying and even the townspeople cannot save it. The girl plants an acorn, hoping it will grow into a grand oak.

After listening to the story, the children revisited their questions. The teacher asked, "What did we learn about trees?" They answered that some trees live as long as people do, but that they do *not* grow back after they are cut. One child made the inference: "Trees can't be protected like animals are, but by planting trees like the girl did you make sure there are always new ones around."

The teacher then asked the final question: "How has your thinking or feeling changed after listening to this story?" The answers were enthusiastic, and included the following:

+ I never really thought about trees before. I just felt like they would always be there.
+ I didn't know trees died like people.
+ I didn't know trees are alive.
+ I know now it takes a long time for a tree to grow.
+ I want to plant some trees too.
+ I appreciate trees more now.

The class then went on a field trip to a local nursery where the nursery owner showed the children many different kinds of trees and explained which grew naturally in their area, which were drought-resistant, and so on. The nursery owner answered questions the children had about trees such as "How can we take care of them?" and "What kills them?"

Back in the classroom, the teacher asked the children: "Which tree is your favorite and why?" Their answers were graphed on chart paper.

As an assignment, children were asked to collect acorns in their neighborhood. Each child planted an acorn in the schoolyard in the following week with teacher supervision.

VIGNETTE 6, GRADE 6.
INTEGRATION: ECOLOGY/SOCIAL STUDIES/READING

The teacher began a lesson on the topic of littering by asking the children: "What are some things people can do to help the problem of littering?" Using a Quick Write[2] (Moore, Readence & Rickelman 1989), they wrote for three minutes.

After sharing their individual responses in small groups, students read Kenneth Lundberg's essay "My Twenty Foot Swatch" to see what one young man's solution was to this pervasive problem.

The teacher put the children in either dyads or triads to share the passage using summarizing and questioning techniques. One pair, John and David, proceeded as follows:

David read two paragraphs aloud.

JOHN (*Summarizing*): The guy in the story asks if we have ever felt so frustrated about world problems that we just did nothing or did something to make it worse. Then he goes on to say he walks across this field every day and notices all the junk that people have thrown on it at soccer games—candy bar wrappers and stuff.

DAVID: Okay—here's my question: If he is so concerned about world problems like pollution, and the environment and everything, why didn't he do something about all that litter?

JOHN: Maybe it would make him late for wherever he's going. I mean, would you pick up somebody else's garbage? Anyway, I think he will do something about it in the next part. (*Reads next two paragraphs aloud.*)

DAVID (*Summarizing*): You're right. He *does* do something about it. First he's so disgusted that he writes letters to people at the newspaper and suggests a clean-up day. But then he decides to do

---

2. Quick Write is a strategy whereby students write everything they can think of about a topic for a short period of time.

it himself. He decides that every day he's going to pick up some litter when he walks back and forth across the field.

JOHN: Did he actually write the letter or was he just thinking about it?

DAVID: Well...(*Reviews the paragraphs.*) Okay, he just was *thinking* to do that but then he thought it wouldn't work anyway and it would probably just raise up his blood pressure. (*Reads next two paragraphs aloud.*)

JOHN (*Summarizing*): He picked up stuff every day, making a game out of it. Finally one day he found out he was picking stuff up faster than the people were littering. First he brought all the garbage home with him. Then some janitor brought some trash cans at each end of the field.

DAVID: Did the janitor do that to help him out or was it just a coincidence?

JOHN: It says the maintenance man was a *conspirator.* I think that means he was helping him out. (*Reads next paragraph.*)

DAVID (*Summarizing*): The guy says he's done this now for a couple of years and the field is not much cleaner and people are still littering. But he says he likes it because it has changed *him.* He is happier and more positive because he's doing something about it.

JOHN: Why wouldn't he still be frustrated if it really isn't changing anything?

DAVID: He just somehow feels he's doing his part. Maybe it will say more about this in the next part. (*Reads next paragraphs.*)

JOHN (*Summarizing*): This guy wants every place he goes to be a little bit better because he was there. Not only cleaning a little litter, but being kind to people and treating everybody he meets as equals.

DAVID: What does this have to do with littering?

JOHN: It's just a piece of all the problems in the world that he was talking about first. He started with littering but then he realized he could do little stuff about *all* the world's problems. (*Reads next paragraphs.*)

DAVID (*Summarizing*): He ends by saying that too many people who speak loudly about world problems care more about being right than really doing anything about them. People should not try to do more than they can do, but they should just do something.

JOHN: Can't you be right and do stuff at the same time? I mean, he *was* right. How can you be too concerned about being right?

DAVID: I think he means they weren't doing enough; they were just talking about it too much. He would think "don't write a letter about it, get out there and do something about the problem yourself!"

After the groups had finished reading the passage, the teacher asked the children to brainstorm the following questions as a whole class:

+ What are some local litter or recycling problems that you know about?
+ What are some general solutions to this problem?
+ What are some individual actions you can take right now?

After much discussion, the children were each asked to sign a contract (see figure 15) committing to whatever individual actions they wished.

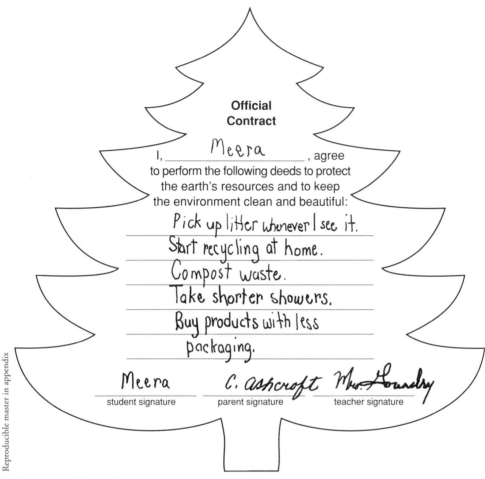

*Figure 15. Official Contract*

## Vignette 7, Grade 4.
### Integration: Science/Social Studies

This fourth-grade teacher wanted to give her students an opportunity to get reactions to one another's questions, because peer perceptions often bring additional insight to questioning behavior. To do this, she presented her students with the following situation:

## Information Sheet

**Name** _Trevor_      **Date** _Oct. 25_

**Names on Panel** _Katie, Alexi, Marc, Jade_

| Question | Judgment & Reason |
|---|---|
| 1. What are the most important things I am bringing, in order of importance? | 1. Good, makes you compare and think about the value. |
| 2. What are some other ways I can use the tea kettle? | 2. Good, leads you to think about other ways to solve the problems. |
| 3. What are some tools I could use to change the tea kettle? | 3. Good, lets you explore the environment. |
| 4. How can I make the food last the longest? | 4. Not great, because it's going to last as long as it's going to last. |
| 5. What will plastic do that canvas can't? | 5. Good, lets you compare the two and find out about properties of plastic. |
| 6. What is the best use for each of these items? | 6. Good. This gets at the most important part of staying alive. |

**Panel's Overall Judgment About Questions**

Their questions will help them to make important decisions about what they need and why. They also will help them to be creative and use the items in ways that they weren't intended to be, which is good because they won't have everything they need.

*Figure 16. Information Sheet*

Reproducible master in appendix

> You are stranded in a wilderness area in the Rocky Mountains for
> two weeks. You have a roll of plastic, a canvas, a tea kettle, a
> flashlight, and some dried fruit.

The teacher explained their chance of survival would depend on specific
courses of action determined by the questions they raised and the answers they received. The focus was not so much on the results, as on the
students' ability to analyze whether or not the questions were or were
not productive (adapted from Hunkins 1978).

Rhe teacher divided the class into groups of three or four and asked
a member in each group to make a list of questions they would ask, reminding them to reflect on why they chose each particular question.
Each group was to evaluate the questions of another group to determine
if their questions were *productive.*

Each panel received an information sheet to record its questions
and its judgments (see figure 16).

## QUESTIONING IN SOCIAL STUDIES

There is no clear consensus among educators about what social studies
in the elementary school ought to be. The emphases vary, according to
the particular proponent, among thinking, knowledge, or good
citizenship. I believe that knowledge and good citizenship can be
obtained best through an integrated curriculum that addresses a variety
of content—historical and current issues—while stimulating the cognitive and affective processes of critical thinking. This can best occur
through effective questioning modeled by teachers and assimilated by
students as in the following examples.

### VIGNETTE 8, GRADE 3.
### INTEGRATION: SOCIAL STUDIES/SCIENCE/ART

Activities that require critical thinking often involve careful observation
and inference, analyzing information in order to draw proper conclu-

sions. The teacher in this example used a mini-inquiry to develop students' capabilities in these areas.

The teacher selected a brief excerpt from the Disney film, *Walk About* (set in the Australian interior), for the children to observe and analyze. Beginning a study of deserts, she used this clip to show key aspects of desert life. The students viewed the clip before having any discussion. They were then asked to draw a rough sketch of some aspect of desert life that particularly stood out to them. When this was completed, the children shared their drawings in pairs, explaining the meaning of each part of their sketch to their partner.

Next the teacher divided the students into small cooperative groups and gave each group a handout with a list of questions to be answered through group consensus. Here are the questions and a sample of group responses:

QUESTION: What are the main characteristics of the desert?

ANSWER: They are hot and dry. There aren't any trees or flowers. Not much lives in the desert. It's cold at night.

Q: What is the name of the native people who live there?

A: Aborigines.

Q: Where in the world is this desert located?

A: In the middle of Australia. Far away from us.

Q: What shelter do these people use?

A: They have houses like us, but not as nice. Little shacks. Some live in caves.

Q: What is their work?

A: Some are guides. Some are hunters. Some raise animals.

Q: What are the most important things in their lives?

A: Finding enough food. Having a happy life. Probably just like us—raising families. Being safe. Staying cool.

Q: How are these people the same as we are?

A: They feel love and hate. They can be happy or sad. They are trying to get by in life. They are humans. They care about other people and their families. They like to laugh and have fun.

Q: How are these people different from us?

A: They don't wear as many clothes. They don't go shopping. Their lives are much harder. They work harder. They speak a different language. They look different.

Q: What are some things we have that they could really use?

A: Television. An air conditioner. A freezer. Ice cream. Ice cubes. A swimming pool. Irrigation.

Q: What question would you like to ask these people?

A: How do you like your life? What do you want to be when you grow up? What do you do for fun? Do you ever want to run away? Do you wish you lived in North America? Do you ever wish you could see snow?

Notice that the questions vary all across the taxonomy—the first are lower level and then they become more critical and open-ended.

After having the children write their preliminary answers, the teacher showed them the clip again, encouraging the groups to rethink and revise their answers as necessary. Then the groups shared their answers, discussing differences in responses and revisiting the tape clip to settle arguments or clarify points. For example, many of the answers offered for the question "What are some things we have that they could really use?" require electricity, which the people in the film do not have. Since these children had never thought about a culture *not* having electricity, they learned something important about their own perceptions. Similarly, for the last question, one group assumed that these desert people would all love to live in the United States or Canada; other groups challenged this assumption and pointed to instances in the tape where they seemed content with their lives.

VIGNETTE 9, GRADE 1.
INTEGRATION: CITIZENSHIP/ROLE PLAYING/ORAL LANGUAGE

During recess, Nelson allegedly pushed Armando to the ground when it was his turn to be up in kickball. Lydia, who saw the whole event, reported it to her teacher. When the teacher asked Nelson what happened during the game, Nelson did not respond. Armando was no longer crying, but he was still upset. Lydia shared that Nelson was probably upset because he had not been allowed to have a turn.

The teacher quickly decided that role-playing was the vehicle through which this unfortunate scenario might be transformed into an authentic social studies/oral language lesson—not just for the two boys involved, but for the entire class. The critical-thinking activity can help children consider the variety of alternative solutions that are available for solving conflict.

The teacher guided her students through the following steps:

1. She had a neutral observer, Lydia, give her version of what had occurred.

2. She selected two children, also neutral, to play the roles of the two children involved.

3. She asked the two actors to take a few minutes to prepare a skit of the incident, exactly as Lydia said it had happened.

4. While the actors prepared the skit, the teacher asked the other children to keep in mind the following questions as they watched the skit:
   + What are the actors doing and saying?
   + How is each feeling?
   + How would you feel if you were either one of the people?
   + What are some other ways this problem could be handled?

5. The teacher reiterated the last question, asking each child to be thinking of one other way the problem could be handled.

6. The children presented their version of the altercation.

7. The audience shared several ideas about other ways the problem might have been handled. The debriefing discussion (excerpted) follows.

TEACHER: What are some other ways that this problem could have been solved? Kristen, Jill, and Craig?

KRISTEN: You could have sent Nelson to the office.

TEACHER: That is true; I could have, but then I would have been taking care of their problem. Can you think of a way they might have solved it themselves?

KRISTEN: Well, Nelson could have come to you and told you that he wasn't getting any turns.

JILL: Or he just could have said that to Armando.

TEACHER: Yes, these are ways that don't hurt anyone. Craig?

CRAIG: He could have just gone away and done something else if they weren't being nice. He didn't have to push somebody.

TEACHER: Those are all different ways to solve the problem. Does anyone have another idea? Brandon?

BRANDON: He could have taken the ball for a minute and made 'em stop the game and said, "Look, you guys, I'm not getting a turn."

TEACHER (*Smiles and nods*): Wow! We thought of lots of different ways that this problem can be solved and no one got pushed down or hurt. Great job!

## VIGNETTE 10, GRADE 6.
### INTEGRATION: GLOBAL AWARENESS/MATH/ WRITING

By using a simulation of food supplies of the world, the children in this sixth-grade class gained a relative perspective of global population groups and food supplies (adapted from Chapin & Messick 1989).

The teacher started off by asking children, "How hungry is the hungriest you have ever been?" She instructed children to do a Quick

Write in response to this question. She then told the children, "We are going to see how much food people have in different parts of the world. We are going to let the children in this class represent all the people in the world."

The teacher then divided the class into five groups proportionately according to the following percentages:

+ *Asia:* 54 percent of the people; 5 percent of the food supply
+ *Africa:* 10 percent of the people; 1 percent of the food supply
+ *Latin America:* 8 percent of the people; 15 percent of the food supply
+ *Middle East:* 2 percent of the people; 5 percent of the food supply
+ *West (United States, Canada, Western Europe):* 26 percent of the people; 74 percent of the food supply

The teacher guided the children to mathematically figure out the proportionate number of children in each of the five groups for their class of thirty. They figured:

Asia: 16 children
Africa: 3 children
Latin America: 2 children
Middle East: 1 child
West: 8 children

The teacher then asked the children to sit in the front of the room with their group, roughly in proportion to their geographical location, as they perceive it on a globe.

Then the teacher brought out a loaf of bread, explaining it represented all the food in the world. She helped the children divide the loaf according to the proportions listed above, by having them calculate the exact portions that each group should have. The bread allotment was then distributed to each group. Children in each group were asked to discuss the following questions, which had been written on the chalkboard:

+ How does your group feel about its food supply?
+ If it is low, could you ask people in other countries to give you some of their food? Why or why not?
+ If it is high, would you consider giving some of it to countries that need more food? Why or why not?
+ Are your responses like the responses of people in the real world? How?

After the groups discussed their answers to the questions, each group shared their ideas with the whole class. Here were some of the children's insights:

WEST: We liked having so much more than everyone else. We definitely think we should share it with other countries. But we think people in the real world in the West—us—don't think very much about how hungry other people are. We just assume everybody has as much as we do.

ASIA: We were really mad at first because we have tons more people than anybody else and not nearly enough to go around. It's not fair. The West should give us some.

MIDDLE EAST: There are groups who have more people than we do and less to eat and less people and more to eat. We're in the middle. We probably have enough, but not enough to give away, but if somebody was starving we would. I don't think the real Mideastern people feel this way, but we don't really know.

TEACHER: What do you think you would like other governments to do about your situation if you do not have enough food? Asia and Africa, I would like you to write to another government and tell them what you have learned. What do you think governments should do if they have *more* than their share of food? West, Middle East, and Latin America, I'd like you to think about this question and write to your *own* government, explaining some ideas you have about how to equalize the world's food supply.

## QUESTIONING IN ART AND MUSIC

The arts seem to be integrally entwined with the need of children to make sense of themselves and their world through symbols. Whereas language is linear and the arts are nonlinear, they are both branches of the same root and can be considered alternative avenues for constructing and conveying meaning. Howard Gardner (1982:5) suggests that through language and the arts the human mind creates, revises, transforms, and "recreates wholly fresh products, systems, and even worlds of meaning." Because of its power to help children think critically and creatively, you need to be aware of how appropriate questioning strategies can help construct meaning in this broad domain as well.

VIGNETTE 11, GRADE 6.
INTEGRATION: ART/SOCIAL STUDIES/WRITING

This sixth-grade class was studying life in ancient Egypt. They were going to make designs on Egyptian urns made of potter's clay, as they had studied in their textbook. Rather than the teacher telling the students about all the proper techniques for making designs on clay, she told them they could experiment with the materials to discover for themselves how to make effective ancient Egyptian pottery designs. Figure 17 shows how one student used a Questioning Sheet to find this out.

VIGNETTE 12, GRADE 4.
INTEGRATION: ART APPRECIATION/MATH/SOCIAL STUDIES

This fourth-grade teacher introduced several famous paintings to her students, and talked about the painter, painter's country of origin, and something about the painter's life. One day, she displayed reproductions of Douglas's *Building More Stately Mansions,* Picasso's *Hand with Flowers,* and Monet's *Water Lilies.* She then asked the children to take a few minutes to really look at the three paintings while thinking about the following questions that she had written on the chalkboard:

+ Which painting speaks to you most? What does it say?
+ What aspect of the painting attracts you?
+ What in your own life does the painting remind you of?

---

**Questioning Sheet**

Name _____Petra_____ Date _Nov. 23_

Project _Making Ancient Egyptian pottery designs_

**Questions I Raised:** What kind of design do I want to make? Do I want it to look a lot like ones in the book or do I want to make something really original? What materials will I need? How long do I have to do this assignment?

**Questions to Which I Responded:** To start off, I answered the first three questions. I sketched an original design and found the clay and the sculpting tool I would use. Then I asked the teacher and he said we have a week to finish our urns.

**My Reactions to the Questions I Asked:** My questions helped me get started by seeing the big picture of what I have to do. They helped me get going.

**Other Questions I Raised As I Worked:** As I was working I wondered how deep should I carve the design? Will too much design make it look bad, or too little make it be boring? What is it about those Egyptian figures and symbols that makes them look Egyptian? I want mine to look realistic.

**My Responses:** I had to answer all those questions. I liked the effect when I carved deep, but it got too messy if I carved too deep. My question about too much or too little design got me to have just the right amount, I think. What makes it look Egyptian, I have decided, is the way the people are all angular and sideways, so I did it that way too, or I tried to anyways.

**My Reactions to My Questions:** My questions helped me to be clear about what I was doing. I felt free to experiment because I told myself why I was doing things.

**Overall Reactions:** I learned a lot this way. I learned about Egyptian urns and pottery, but I also learned about how I feel about it. I'd like to do it again and try it a different way.

(Adapted from F. P. Hunkins' *Involving Students in Questioning*, 1978: 181–182.)

*Figure 17. Questioning Sheet*

+ What are some places, people, or images that the painting brings to your mind?
+ What would you change about the painting? Why?
+ Write down some words and open-ended phrases that express some of the feelings you have about this painting.

To illustrate how these questions might be answered, the teacher selected the painting that spoke to *her* the most, and mused aloud what the painting reminded her of in her life, just how it affected her, and even what she would like to change about the painting.

When the children had had time to reflect upon their feelings and reactions to one of the paintings, they were asked to search for a partner who had chosen a painting different from the one they had chosen.

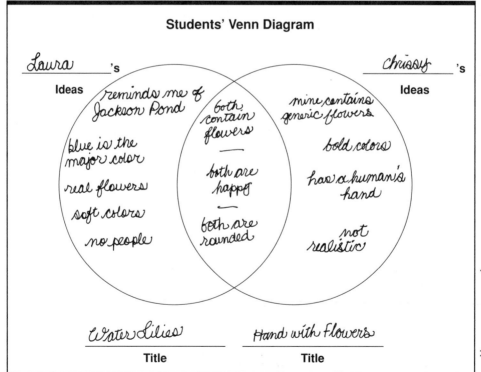

**Students' Venn Diagram**

Laura _____'s    Chrissy _____'s
Ideas    Ideas

reminds me of Jackson Pond

blue is the major color

real flowers

soft colors

no people

both contain flowers

—

both are happy

—

both are rounded

mine contains generic flowers

bold colors

has a human's hand

not realistic

Water Lilies
**Title**

Hand with Flowers
**Title**

*Figure 18. Students' Venn Diagram*

(For example, one child with a dark favorite painting may decide to team up with a child who has chosen a bright favorite painting.)

The two children then sat together and, using their responses to the questions, made a Venn diagram to graphically illustrate the similarities and dissimilarities in the two paintings (see figure 18). They then used the Venn diagram as a prop to discuss their feelings about the paintings with the rest of the class.

VIGNETTE 13, GRADE 2.
INTEGRATION: MUSIC/WRITING

Children in a grade-two class were able to write their reactions to music using a contrast frame (Cudd 1990). This device provides a literacy scaffold, or temporary structure, for the children to use so that they may begin to record their observations in an expository mode. (A contrast frame can be used by a group or individually.) While such a device is useful in helping children to organize their ideas, it is especially helpful for children for whom English is a second language, as they begin to acquire literacy skills.

The teacher selected two pieces of classical music that are very different from one another: Grieg's "Morning," and Grieg's "The Hall of the Mountain King," both from the *Peer Gynt Suite.* After listening to each piece, the teacher asked the children to respond to the following questions:

+ What does this music remind you of?
+ How does it make you feel?
+ What do you see in your mind when you hear this music?
+ What does the music make you want to do?

After *both* pieces had been discussed using the above questions, the teacher asked the children the following questions:

+ How are these two pieces of music different?
+ How are they the same?
+ In what way are they *most* different?

A contrast frame was then used to summarize the differences between the two pieces of music. It was completed by the teacher, using the responses offered by a small group of children.

"The Hall of the Mountain King" and "Morning" differ in several ways. First, "The Hall of the Mountain King" is _scary_, while "Morning" is _calm_. Second, "The Hall of the Mountain King" is _fast_, while "Morning" is _gentle and slow_. Probably the way the two pieces of music are _most_ different is _that "Hall of the Mountain King" is loud and makes me go crazy_, while _"Morning"_ is soft and makes me feel all peaceful.

(Adapted from Cecil & Lauritzen 1994)

*Figure 19. Contrast Frame*

# SUMMARY OF PART II

Questioning is one of the most essential functions of teaching. Critical and creative questions, well-planned and sequenced, stimulate higher cognitive achievements and make information more meaningful. If these generally accepted assertions are valid, then teachers must achieve a high degree of sensitivity, awareness, and skill in using questioning techniques in the most effective and appropriate manner.

Chapters 3 and 4 provided you with questioning strategies and activities to stimulate the highest critical and creative thinking skills, by inviting the learners to become totally engaged in the process. If learning can be made meaningful and relevant, students will enjoy working at it.

The questioning strategies in these chapters provided you with important tools of the trade. But remember they are just that—tools. Each technique must be used appropriately and must be congruent with the objectives that you have for a specific individual, small group, or large class. Finally, it is important that the questioning sessions in classrooms center around worthwhile content leading to constructive and joyful experiences where all children's thoughts and opinions are respected, their interests stimulated, and their minds challenged.

Volumes have been written about what makes children become proficient readers, or readers who are able to construct meaning from text. To briefly summarize these studies, five important strategies emerge that are typical of competent readers and thinkers.

1. They are able to generate questions about text.

2. They are able to summarize.

3. They are able to make predictions.

4. They are able to find important information.

5. They are able to monitor their own understanding of text.

Chapters 5 and 6 explored strategies that can be taught to children to show them how asking their own questions can help them construct meaning from text. Each of the strategies, additionally, can enhance students' abilities in at least one of the five important skills just listed: Dyad Reading and Schema-General Questions assist students in summarizing; Survey, Question, Read, Recite, and Review (SQ3R), Self-Instruction, and Question-Generating Questions are helpful in showing children how to ask appropriate questions; Basal Reader Prediction Strategy can help readers learn to predict text; I-Search and Question-Answer Relationships (QARs) aid students, through questioning, to find important information in text; and both Cognitive Instruction Strategy in Writing (CISW) and the Metacognitive Strategy offer children insights into how they can more effectively monitor their own understanding as they are reading and writing.

In chapter 7, we looked at how questions can help children understand content and make clear connections across the entire elementary curriculum. Children are natural meaning-makers, always attempting to make sense of their world. Because they are active, constructive learners, they are constantly solving problems, generating and testing hypotheses. Because their hypotheses may be confirmed or disclaimed at any time, risk-taking is inherent in this ever-changing process of learning. Moreover, the hypotheses that are made are usually about some specific topic, a specific domain of knowledge. Hypotheses are rarely content-free. Therefore, what children know—their schema for a specific topic of study—and the new knowledge to which you guide them, can be the foundation upon which critical questions are formulated.

· · · ·

# Conclusion

I believe that teaching and questioning are indelibly linked; a notion
that is a driving premise of this book. A program of excellent teaching has to, in some way, involve questioning—the teacher's chief
means of channeling and stimulating discourse.

The type of teaching I advocate, however, is not congruent with
only "know-the-answer-beforehand" questions; you also have to ask
questions for which there are no "right" answers. It helps, therefore, to
be aware of the various types of questions that exist so that you are able
to deliberately form questions appropriate to the context and content
of the material as well as for the ability of your students. By varying the
questions, you can then elicit a wide range of responses, thereby developing in your students a broad range of cognitive and affective skills
they need for independent thinking. And, since you know neither the
answer nor exactly what to expect from your students when asking such
questions, you must remain totally vigilant and intellectually involved
throughout the entire lesson. This is a most exciting challenge!

When you engage in this type of questioning, you do far more
than simply interact with your students—something traditional-ques-
tioning strategists often overlook. First, you summarize and sharpen
responses and reactions by rephrasing them, thus spotlighting essential
points made by students. Second, you play "discussion traffic cop": you
call upon children who wish to speak while requesting that others listen
cautiously and comment thoughtfully on the ideas on the floor. Third,
by making it clear you are not expecting one "right" answer to your
questions, you encourage multiple responses and recitations. Because
you do much more than merely question, you often rely on more than
just the asking of questions to bring out ideas. Ideas are generated from

student responses, and through your own remarks and comments. Therefore, it is not always possible to know ahead of time exactly which question you will ask next. Finally, when you use open-ended questions for which you have no clearly defined answer, you eliminate the pointless game whereby students anxiously attempt to figure out what is in your mind. Instead, you and your students are thrust into roles as "co-inquirers." For the student, this means responsibility, accountability, and above all, profound intellectual stimulation. For you, this means assuming the role of guide to the student as you provide a model of an inquisitive adult exploring new ground.

Provoking students to do the questioning—both of you and of each other—is perhaps the most significant task you face. Clearly, students must learn to question as well as respond if they are to become independent thinkers. To encourage student questioning, you must directly invite student questions, comments, and even, at times, criticisms! Also, you must establish a safe atmosphere in any discourse so that students feel totally free to express themselves without fear of reprisal from you or the other students. You will find the questions students ask arise from an earnest desire to understand both the topic at hand and the position taken by their classmates, rather than as a means to gain your favor.

The most effective technique for encouraging student questioning has been the linchpin of the book; you, the teacher, must establish yourself as a curious, knowledge-seeking role model whom the students yearn to emulate. As such, it is important to not only ask many different kinds of questions, but also to respectfully consider the host of questions generated by your students.

All the teachers you have met in this book represent attributes and attitudes about learning that I have seen in real classrooms in real teachers who used questioning techniques successfully. These teachers have demonstrated a broad spectrum of choices of activities for children to engage in and they have shown an infectious curiosity and love for learning.

Perhaps the most salient characteristic of the teachers in this book is the way they collaborate with children through the use of their questions. In the vignettes in chapter 7, for example, the teachers posed questions for children to consider, supported children's hypotheses about possible solutions for their own problems, facilitated children's own question-raising, and affirmed their struggles with ideas. These teachers realize that knowledge is not just about facts or absolute truths to be poured into the minds of children as if they were empty vessels; they are well aware that children construct their own knowledge, their own theories about the world.

There is, of course, no magic formula for teaching. But I believe for learning to be important to the lives of children, teachers must be caring, committed, and ready to ignite the sparks of interest in children through modeling questions and helping children to ask their *own* questions. The purpose of this book has been to help you be that kind of teacher.

. . . .

# REFERENCES

Anderson, C. W., and E. L. Smith. "Teaching Science." In *Educators' Handbook*. Edited by V. Richardson-Koehler. White Plains, NY: Longman, 1987.

Angletti, S. R. "Encouraging Students to Think About What They Read." *Reading Teacher* 45 (1991): 288–296.

Armbruster, B. "Content Area Reading Instruction." A presentation given at the Conference on Reading Research, CORR, Las Vegas, NV, 1991a.

Armbruster, B. "Reading and Questioning in Content Area Lessons." *Journal of Reading Behavior* 23 (1991b): 35–39.

Ashton-Warner, S. *Spearpoint.* New York: Vintage, 1974.

Au, K. "Using the Experience-Text-Relationship Method with Minority Children." *Reading Teacher* 32 (1979): 478–79.

Baker, L., and A. L. Brown. "Metacognitive Skills and Reading." In *Handbook of Reading Research,* 353–394. Edited by P. D. Pearson. New York: Longman, 1984.

Balajthy, E. "The Relationship of Training of Self-Generated Questioning with Passage Difficulty and Immediate and Delayed Retention." Paper presented at the American Educational Research Association, Montreal, PQ, 1983.

Bird, L. "Reading Comprehension Redefined Through Literature Study: Creating Worlds from the Printed Page." *California Reader* 21 (1988): 9–14.

Blank, M., and D. Allen. "Understanding 'Why': Its Significance in Early Intelligence." In *Origins of Intelligence*, 259–278. Edited by M. Lewis. New York: Plenum, 1976.

Bleich, D. *Subjective Criticism.* Baltimore, MD: John Hopkins University Press, 1978.

Bloom, B. S., ed. *Taxonomy of Educational Objectives.* White Plains, NY: Longman, 1984.

Bromley, K. D. *Language Arts: Exploring Connections.* 2nd edition. Boston: Allyn & Bacon, 1992.

Buckley, M. H. "When Teachers Decide to Integrate the Language Arts." *Language Arts* 63 (1986): 369–377.

Carin, A. A., and R. B. Sund. *Developing Questioning Techniques: A Self-Concept Approach.* Columbus, OH: Merrill, 1991.

Cecil, N. L. *Freedom Fighters: Affective Teaching of the Language Arts.* Salem, WI: Sheffield, 1994.

———. *Teaching to the Heart: Affective Teaching of Literacy.* Salem, WI: Sheffield, 1993.

———. "Where Have All the Good Questions Gone? Encouraging Creative Expression in Children." In *Literacy in the '90s: Selected Readings in the Language Arts.* Edited by N. L. Cecil. Dubuque, IA: Kendall/Hunt, 1990.

Cecil, N. L., and P. Lauritzen. *Literacy and the Arts for the Integrated Classroom: Alternative Ways of Knowing.* White Plains, NY: Longman, 1994.

Chapin, J. R., and R. G. Messick. *Elementary Social Studies: A Practical Guide,* 129–130. White Plains, NY: Longman, 1989.

Cooper, J. D. *Literacy: Helping Children Construct Meaning.* Boston: Houghton Mifflin, 1993.

Cornbleth, C. "Student Questioning as a Learning Strategy." *Educational Leadership* 33 (1975): 219–222.

Costa, A. L. *The School Is a Home for the Mind.* Palatine, IL: Skylight, 1991.

Cudd, E. "The Paragraph Frame: A Bridge from Narrative to Expository Text." In *Literacy in the '90s: Selected Readings in the Language Arts.* Edited by N. L. Cecil. Dubuque, IA: Kendall/Hunt, 1990.

Davey, B. "Think-Aloud: Modeling the Cognitive Processes of Reading Comprehension." *Journal of Reading* 27 (1983): 44–47.

Davidman, Leonard. *Teaching with a Multicultural Perspective: A Practical Guide.* New York: Longman, 1994.

Eberle, R. F. *Scamper On.* Buffalo, NY: DOK Publishers, 1984.

Edelsky, C. "Living in the Author's World: Analyzing the Author's Craft." *California Reader* 21 (1988): 15–22.

Floyd, W. D. "An Analysis of the Oral Questioning Activity in Selected Colorado Primary Classrooms." Unpublished doctoral dissertation, Colorado State University, 1960.

Galda, L., B. E. Cullinan, and D. S. Strickland. *Language Literacy and the Child.* Orlando, FL: Harcourt Brace Jovanovich, 1993.

Gardner, H. *Art, Mind, and Brain: A Cognitive Approach to Creativity.* New York: Basic Books, 1982.

Hunkins, F. P. *Questioning Strategies and Techniques.* Boston: Allyn & Bacon, 1972.

———. *Involving Students in Questioning.* Boston: Allyn & Bacon, 1978.

Hyde, A. A., and M. Bizar. *Thinking in Context: Teaching Cognitive Processes Across the Elementary School Curriculum.* White Plains, NY: Longman, 1989.

Kestler, J. L. *Questioning Techniques and Tactics.* Boston: Allyn & Bacon, 1992.

Konapale, B. C., S. H. Martin, and M. A. Martin. "Using a Writing Strategy to Enhance Sixth-Grade Students' Comprehension of Material." *Journal of Reading Behavior* 22 (1990): 19–37.

Langer, J., A. Applebee, I. Mullis, and M. Foertsch. "Learning to Read in Our Nation's Schools: Instruction and Achievement in 1988 at Grades 4, 8 and 12." In *National Assessment of Educational Progress.* Princeton, NY: Educational Testing Service, 1990.

Mason, J. M., and K. M. Au. *Reading Instruction for Today.* Glenview, IL: Scott Foresman, 1986.

McNeil, J. D. *Reading Comprehension: New Directions for Classroom Practice.* Glenview, IL: Scott Foresman, 1984.

MERIT, Chapter 2 Project. *Developing Metacognitive Skills.* Philadelphia: School District of Philadelphia, 1986.

Moore, D. W., J. E. Readence, and R. J. Rickelman. *Prereading Activities for Content Area Reading and Learning.* 2nd edition. Newark, DE: International Reading Association, 1989.

Ogle, D. "K-W-L: A Teaching Model that Develops Active Reading of Expository Text." *Reading Teacher* 39 (1986): 564–570.

Orlich, D. C., R. C. Callahan, C. H. Kravas, D. P. Kauchak, R. A. Pendergrass, and J. K. Andrews. *Teaching Strategies: A Guide to Better Instruction.* Lexington, MA: D. C. Heath, 1985.

Palinscar, A.M., and A.L. Brown. "Reciprocal Teaching of Comprehension." *Cognition and Instruction* 1 (1984): 117–175.

Pressley, M., J. Barkell, T. Cariglia-Bull, L. Lysynchuck, J. A. McGoldrick, B. Schneider, B. L. Snyder, S. Symons, and V. E. Woloshyn. *Cognitive Strategy Instruction that Really Improves Children's Academic Performance.* Cambridge, MA: Brookline, 1990.

Raphael, T. E. "Question-Answering Strategies for Children." *Reading Teacher* 36 (1982): 186–190.

Raphael, T. E., and C. S. Englebert. "Writing and Reading: Partners in Constructing Meaning." *Reading Teacher* 43 (1990): 388–400.

Robinson, F. P. *Effective Study.* Revised edition. New York: Harper & Row, 1961.

Rogers, D. L. "Are Questions the Answer?" *Dimensions* 19 (1990): 3–5.

Sigel, I. E. "The Relationship Between Parental Distancing Strategies and the Child's Cognitive Behavior." In *Families as Learning Environments for Children,* 47–86. Edited by L. Laosa and I. Sigel. New York: Plenum, 1982.

Sigel, I. E., and R. Saunders. "An Inquiry Into Inquiry: Question Asking as an Instructional Model." In *Current Topics in Early Childhood,* Vol. 2, 169–193. Edited by L. Katz. Norwood, NJ: Ablex, 1979.

Singer, H. "Active Comprehension: From Answering to Asking Questions." *Reading Teacher* 31 (1978): 901–908.

Singer, H., and D. Donlon. "Active Comprehension: Problem-Solving Schema with Question Generation for Comprehension of Complex Short Stories." *Reading Research Quarterly* 17 (1982): 166–187.

Thomas, D. K. "*Why* Questions and *Why* Answers: Patterns and Purposes." *Language Arts* 65 (1988): 552–556.

Tierney, R. J., J. E. Readence, and E. K. Dishner. *Reading Strategies and Practices.* 2nd edition. Boston: Allyn & Bacon: 1985.

Wendler, D., S. J. Samuels, and V. Moore. "The Comprehension Instruction of Award-Winning Teachers, Teachers with Master's Degrees, and Other Teachers." *Reading Research Quarterly* 24 (1989): 382–401.

Wood, K. D. "Probable Passages: A Writing Strategy." *Reading Teacher* 37 (1987): 496–499.

Yamomoto, K. *Teaching.* Boston: Houghton Mifflin, 1969.

Yopp, R. H., and H. K. Yopp. *Literature-based Reading Activities.* Boston: Allyn & Bacon, 1992.

. . . .

# SUGGESTED READING

Albriton, T. "Honest Questions and the Teaching of English." *English Education* 24 (1992): 91–100.

Armbruster, B. "On Answering Questions (Reading to Learn)." *Reading Teacher* 45 (1992): 724–725.

Ash, B. H. "Student-made Questions: One Way into a Literacy Text." *English Journal* 81 (1992): 61–64.

Baloche, L., L. Platt, and J. Thomas. "Sprouting Magic Beans: Creative Questioning and Cooperative Learning." *Language Arts* 70 (1993): 264–271.

Beck, I., and M. G. McKeown. "Developing Questions that Promote Comprehension: The Story Map." *Language Arts* 58 (1981): 913–917.

Benito, Y. M., et al. "The Effect of Instruction in Question-Answer Relationships and Metacognition on Social Studies Comprehension." *Journal of Research in Reading* 16 (1993): 20–29.

Camp, W. G. "Improving Your Teaching: Questioning Techniques." *Agricultural Education* 66 (1993): 17–23.

Carlsen, W. S. "Questioning in Classrooms: A Sociolinguistic Perspective." *Review of Educational Research* 61 (1991): 157–178.

Carr, W., and S. Kemmis. *Becoming Critical.* London: The Falmer Press, 1986.

Christenbury, L., and P. P. Kelly. *Questioning: A Critical Path to Critical Thinking.* Urbana, IL: ERIC Clearinghouse on Reading and Communications Skills and the National Council of Teachers of English, 1983. (NIE 400-78-0026)

Clarke, D., and P. Sullivan. "Is a Question the Best Answer?" *Australian Mathematics Teacher* 46 (1990): 30–33.

Clegg, A. A. "Classroom Questions." In *The Encyclopedia of Education*, Vol. 2. New York: Macmillan, 1971.

Commetras, M. "Analyzing a Critical-Thinking Reading Lesson." *Teaching and Teacher Education* 6 (1990): 201–214.

Daines, D. *Teachers' Oral Questions and Subsequent Verbal Behavior of Teachers and Students.* Provo, UT: Brigham Young University, 1982. (ERIC Document Reproduction Service No. ED 225 979)

Dillon, J. T. "Do Your Questions Promote or Prevent Thinking?" *Learning* 11 (1982): 56–57.

———. "A Norm Against Student Questions." *The Clearing House* 55 (1981a): 135–139.

———. "To Question or Not to Question During Discussions." *Journal of Teacher Education* 32 (1981b): 51–55.

Dole, J., et al. "Moving from the Old to the New: Research on Reading Comprehension Instruction." *Review of Educational Research* 61 (1991): 239–264.

Dupuis, M. M., ed. *Reading in the Content Areas: Research for Teachers.* Newark, DE: International Reading Association, 1984.

Fishbein, H. D., et al. "Learners' Questions and Comprehension in a Tutorial Setting." *Journal of Educational Psychology* 82 (1990): 163–170.

Freedman, A. "Adapting the I-Search Paper for the Elementary Classroom." In *Practical Ideas for Teaching Writing as a Process*, 114–116. Edited by C. B. Olson. Sacramento: California State Department of Education, 1986.

Gilbert, S. W. "Systematic Questioning: Taxonomies that Develop Critical Thinking Skills." *Science Teacher* 59 (1992): 41–46.

Jenkins, C., and D. Lawler. "Questioning Strategies in Content Area Reading: One Teacher's Example." *Reading Improvement* 27 (1990): 133–138.

Johnson, B. E. "Concept Question Chain: A Framework for Thinking and Learning About Text." *Reading Horizons* 32 (1992): 263–278.

Johnson, K. M., et al. "Use of Modeling to Enhance Children's Interrogative Strategies." *Journal of School Psychology* 29 (1991): 81–88.

Johnson, N. "Questioning Etiquette." *Gifted Child Today* 13 (1990): 10–11.

Karmos, J. S., et al. "Questioning Techniques for the Classroom." *Illinois Schools Journal* 69 (1990): 20–24.

King, A. "Enhancing Peer Interaction and Learning in the Classroom Through Reciprocal Questioning." *American Educational Research Journal* 27 (1990): 647–687.

Knapczyk, D. "Effects of Modeling on Promoting Generalization of Student Question Asking and Answering." *Learning Disabilities Research and Practice* 6 (1991): 75–82.

Land, M. L. "Teacher Clarity and Cognitive Level of Questions: Effects on Learning." *Journal of Experimental Education* 49(1980): 48–51.

Leeds, D. "The Art of Asking Questions." *Training and Development* 47 (1993): 57–58, 60–62.

Leggo, C. "The Reader as Problem-Maker: Responding to a Poem with Questions." *English Journal* 80 (1991): 58–60.

Lyons, C. "The Use of Questions in the Teaching of High-Risk Beginning Readers: A Profile of a Developing Reading Recovery Teacher." *Reading and Writing Quarterly: Overcoming Learning Difficulties* 9 (1993): 317–327.

Marzano, R. J. "How Classroom Teachers Approach the Teaching of Thinking." *Theory into Practice* 32 (1993): 154–160.

Neilsen, Lorri. *A Stone in My Shoe: Teaching Literacy in Times of Change.* Winnipeg, MB: Peguis, 1994.

O'Malley, J. L. "Asking the Right Questions." *Social Studies* 81 (1990): 89–91.

Otto, P. B. "Finding an Answer in Questioning Strategies." *Science and Children* 28 (1991): 44–47.

Proudfit, L. "Questioning in the Elementary Mathematics Classroom." *School Science and Mathematics* 92 (1992): 133–135.

Riley, J. "The Answer to the Question Is to Listen to the Answer: An Evaluation of Teacher-Student Interaction During Discussions Preparatory to Reading." *Reading World* 22 (1982): 26–33.

Ring, A. "Effects of Training in Strategic Questioning on Children's Problem-Solving Performance." *Journal of Educational Psychology* 83 (1991): 307–317.

Roller, C. "Classroom Interaction Patterns: Reflections of a Stratified Society." *Language Arts* 66 (1989): 492–500.

Ryder, R. J. "The Directed Questioning Activity for Subject Matter Text." *Journal of Reading* 34 (1991): 606–612.

Shiang, C., and E. McDaniel. "Examining the Effects of Questioning on Thinking Processes with a Computer-Based Exercise." *Journal of Educational Computing Research* 7 (1991): 203–217.

Sternberg, R. J. "Answering Questions and Questioning Answers: Guiding Children to Intellectual Excellence." *Phi Delta Kappan* 76 (1994): 136–138.

Thomas, B. B. "How Can We Use What We Know About Questioning Skills to Develop Literate Thinkers?" *Reading Horizons* 33 (1992): 19–30.

Tompkins, G. E., and K. Hoskisson. *Language Arts: Content and Teaching Strategies.* New York: Merrill, 1991.

Van der Meij, H. "What's the Title? A Case of Study of Questioning in Reading." *Journal of Research in Reading* 16 (1993): 46–56.

Wasserman, S. "Teaching Strategies: The Art of the Question." *Childhood Education* 67 (1991): 257–259.

Wing, L. A. "The Interesting Questions Approach to Learning." *Childhood Education* 69 (1992): 78–81.

Young, T. A., and D. Daines. "Students' Predictive Questions and Teachers' Prequestions About Expository Text in Grades K–5." *Reading Psychology* 13 (1992): 291–308.

. . . .

# LITERATURE CITED

Asbjornsen, Peter Christen. *The Three Billy Goats Gruff.* New York: Harcourt Brace, 1957.

Barrie, J. M. *Peter Pan.* New York: Children's Classics, 1987.

Bawden, Nina. *The Outside Child.* New York: Puffin, 1994; New York: Lothrop, Shepard Books, 1989.

Birchall, Brian. *Kahu, the Cautious Kiwi.* Aukland: (A New Zealand Golden Book), 1990.

Bunting, Eve. *Someday a Tree.* New York: Clarion, 1993.

Saunders, Susan. *Puss in Boots.* New York: Scholastic, 1989.

Komaiko, Leah. *Earl's Too Cool for Me.* New York: HarperCollins, 1988.

Lundberg, Kenneth. "My Twenty Foot Swatch." In *Saving the Earth.* Edited by C. Franck. Philadelphia: Covenant Press, 1982.

Nader, C. J. *Pegasus the Winged Horse.* Mahwah: Troll, 1981.

Paulsen, Gary. *A Christmas Sonata.* New York: Delacorte, 1992.

Rylant, Cynthia. *Miss Maggie.* New York: Dutton, 1988.

Wilhelm, Hans. *Bunny Trouble.* New York: Scholastic, 1985.

Williams, Jay. *The Practical Princess.* New York: Parents' Magazine Press, 1969.

"Young Man with a Mission: Albert Schweitzer." In *Adventures with World Heroes.* Edited by R. L. Whitehead. Chicago: Benefic Press, 1979.

. . . .

# APPENDIX:
# REPRODUCIBLE MASTERS

# The Knowledge Chart

**Name** _____  **Date** _____

**Topic** _____

| Knowledge | Questions | New Knowledge | Research | Reactions |
|---|---|---|---|---|
| What do you know about _____ ? | What do you want to know about _____ ? | What did you discover after reading about _____ ? | What do you still want to know about _____ ? | How do you now think or feel about _____ ? |

Figure 6, page 47, The Knowledge Chart

# Response Heuristic

**Name** _____ **Date** _____

**Book Title** _____

1. What is important in the book?

2. How does the story make you feel?

3. What experiences have you had that the story reminds you of?

From *The Art of Inquiry* by Nancy Lee Cecil © 1995.
This page may be photocopied for classroom use. Note: photocopy at 135% for actual size.

Figure 7, page 50, Response Heuristic

## Probable Passages: Postreading Stage

**Name** _____ **Date** _____

**Book Title** _____

### Revised Probable Passage

The story takes place _____

_____ .

_____ is a character in the story who

_____

_____ .

A problem occurs when _____

_____

_____

_____ .

Then _____

_____

_____ .

The problem is solved when _____

_____

_____

_____ .

The story ends _____

_____

_____

_____ .

Figure 9c, page 62, Probable Passages

156

---

## Think Aloud

**Name** _____ **Date** _____

**Story Title** _____

1. How often did I ask myself what I thought this story or paragraph was about?

    never     sometimes     often     after every paragraph

2. How often did I see pictures in my mind of what was going on?

    never     sometimes     often     after every paragraph

3. How often did what I read remind me of something else that I know about?

    never     sometimes     often     after every paragraph

4. How often did I stop to see if I was understanding what was going on in the story or paragraph?

    never     sometimes     often     after every paragraph

5. How often did I change what I had originally thought about what was going on in the story or passage?

    never     sometimes     often     after every paragraph

Figure 10, page 67, Think Aloud

# SCAMPERing

**Name** _____ **Date** _____

**Book Title** _____

To rewrite the story in a new way, select a question, then answer it in the
space at the bottom (turn the page if you need more room).

1. **Substitute:**

2. **Combine:**

3. **Adapt:**

4. **Modify:**

5. **Magnify:**

6. **Put to Use:**

7. **Point of View:**

8. **Eliminate:**

9. **Rearrange:**

10. **Reverse:**

**Answer:** _____

_____

_____

_____

_____

_____

Figure 11, page 76, SCAMPERing

# Schema-General Questions

**Name** _____  **Date** _____

**Book Title** _____

Using the questions you have learned to ask yourself,
write a summary of the book under the following headings.

The Main Character

The Goal

The Problem

The Resolution

The Theme

Figure 12, page 94, Schema-General Questions

| I-Search | | |
|---|---|---|
| **Name** _____ **Date** _____ | | |
| **Question** _____ | | |
| **What do I already know?** | *Information:* | |
| **How do I find the information I need?** | *Sources:* | *What the Sources Said:* |
| | | |
| **What did I discover?** | | |

Figure 13, page 99, I-Search

---

## CSIW

**Name** _____ **Date** _____

**Topic** _____

**What** is my topic?


**Who** am I writing for?


**What** do I already know about this topic?


**Where** can I get more information on this topic?


**What** organizational structure should I use?


**What** are some beginning ideas?


**What** are some ending ideas?

---

Figure 14, page 104, CSIW

**Official
Contract**

I, _____ , agree
to perform the following deeds to protect
the earth's resources and to keep
the environment clean and beautiful:

_____

_____

_____

_____

_____

_____

_____   _____   _____
student signature    parent signature    teacher signature

Figure 15, page 123, Official Contract

## Information Sheet

Name _____     Date _____

Names on Panel _____

| Question | Judgment & Reason |
|---|---|
|  |  |

**Panel's Overall Judgment About Questions**

Figure 16, page 124, Information Sheet

## Questioning Sheet

Name _____ Date _____

Project _____

**Questions I Raised:**

**Questions to Which I Responded:**

**My Reactions to the Questions I Asked:**

**Other Questions I Raised As I Worked:**

**My Responses:**

**My Reactions to My Questions:**

**Overall Reactions:**

(Adapted from F. P. Hunkins' *Involving Students in Questioning,* 1978: 181–182.)

Figure 17, page 133, Questioning Sheet

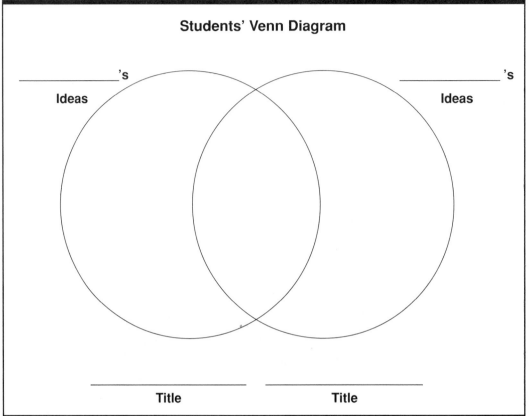

Figure 18, page 134, Venn Diagram